Paper Thin

Paper Thin: A Memoir

Copyright © 2018 by Justine Domagall.

All rights reserved. Printed in the United States of America. No part of this book may be used or reproduced in any manner whatsoever without written permission.

ISBN: 0-578-46533-7

First Edition: 2019

Cover photo and design by Grace Gelineau

For my parents—who fought for me when
I didn't have the strength to fight for myself

Preface

Dear reader,

I believe that things happen for a reason, but I don't view God as a puppeteer sitting up in heaven controlling how things play out on earth. I don't believe God caused me to get sick. I don't believe my parents caused it either. I think it was the perfect storm of a perfectionistic personality, a brain hardwired to overthink, and the normal stresses of life. Could God have prevented it from happening? Probably. But maybe sometimes, like any good parent, he lets us deal with the consequences of our actions. Then, when it's over, he helps us pick up the pieces and turn something broken into something beautiful.

Maybe you're reading this because you struggle with an eating disorder yourself, or maybe you love someone who is going through this struggle. Either way, I'm glad you've picked up this book. This is not a self-help book. It's not a guide for getting rid of an eating disorder. But my hope is that by reading this you will better understand how the disease works. How it takes hold of an individual and changes the way they think, feel, and behave. How it can transform you or your loved one into something they never were and never wanted to be.

Every professional I've worked with or spoken to who treats eating disorders refers to the disease as an entity separate from the person. Sometimes the disease is even given a name like "Ed" (for eating disorder) or "Anna" (for anorexia). This may seem a little strange, but it makes it easier to remember the separation. You or your loved one are not your or their eating disorder. I cannot stress this enough. You will notice as you read that some of my entries contradict each other. Sometimes they even seem to be written by different people. This is me switching back and forth from writing as myself versus through the lens of the eating disorder. Even when I was at my worst there were times, mainly while writing, that I could see the eating disorder for what it was and what it was doing to me. Those moments of clarity, no matter how short, kept me alive.

Before you begin reading, there are some things I want to note. First, this book does not include all of my journal entries during the time period covered. If it did it would be the size of a dictionary. I cut out most of the entries regarding random life events not related to the eating disorder. My hope is that the book still flows well and is understandable. Second, there are a few details I either changed or took out. Any mention of what I weighed, for example, is blacked out. There is no such thing as one healthy weight. Everyone's healthy weight range is determined by a number of personal factors, and I don't want anyone to fixate on my own numbers which mean nothing to them. I also changed names and identifying information of anyone not in my immediate family. And, lastly, you will notice that, especially near the end of the book, my entries become more spiritually focused. Initially I wondered about this. My concern was that it would deter readers who are not spiritual themselves. But then I realized that if I took out my spirituality, my faith, my relationship with God, then there would be no story of recovery. My story would end with me wasting away while the people who loved me watched but could do nothing about it.

I've been asked before whether I would change what happened if I could. The honest answer is yes. I'd change it because of the people I hurt while I was sick. I never intended to hurt them, and I deeply regret doing so. At the same time, I can acknowledge the good that eventually came from the struggle. My family and I are closer than we've ever been. I also got the help I needed for depression and anxiety, which might have otherwise gone untreated if the eating disorder hadn't made it obvious that something was wrong.

And you, readers, are the other good that might come from it. My hope is that you will not walk away from this book unchanged but instead will gain insight and, most importantly, hope. This fight is a difficult one, but you don't have to do it alone. There are others who have fought through it and made it out on the other side. I used to think that I'd never be free from the eating disorder. That no matter how much I fought there would always be some part of it with me, but that wasn't the case and it doesn't have to be for you either. There is freedom.

May God bless you and give you strength as you fight this battle.

Justine

May 21, 2009

I've never been good at keeping a journal or diary or whatever you want to call it. It's not that I don't have enough to write about or the time to write. There are two main reasons. The first is simple. I write too much. I go into too much detail and can't keep up with the dates because each time I come back to write I end up trying to finish the entry from the day before. The second, and more important reason, is that I'm a perfectionist. I want everything to be perfect including my writing. Perfection, unfortunately, is rarely possible, especially with writing. My mind is a mess sometimes. The whole point of writing is to transfer my thoughts onto paper, so if I'm going to truly do that my writing will also (sometimes) be a mess. This drives me completely crazy, but for now I'm just going to have to deal with it. No ripping out pages and no writing in pencil because there is no erasing. None. This is going to be extremely hard for me, but I'm just going to do it because these thoughts need paper no matter how messy they are.

May 22, 2009

I am so frustrated right now. Actually, I'm frustrated most of the time. This is my body, my life, so why am I not in control of it? Why does everyone else get to decide what I eat, where I go, and I have no say in it?

They say I'm unhealthy. I'm not providing my body with the energy it needs. My heart rate is too low because the lack of food is making my organs shrink. I'm at risk for heart failure and permanent organ damage. I haven't gotten my period in over six months. My bones are shrinking, becoming brittle, and it's more likely that I will break or fracture one maybe even just from putting too much pressure on it. That's what they're saying, but do I believe them? Other than not getting my period everything else seems fine. And maybe the loss of my period has nothing to do with food. Maybe my reproductive organs were already messed up.

I don't know what to believe anymore. The doctors have classified it as anorexia. I don't see it, don't believe it, but the doctors also say that denial is one of the symptoms. People with anorexia don't think that they have it. They don't think that they have a problem, and that's why it is one of the hardest diseases to cure. A normal illness would be easier because at least the person who has it would be trying to get rid of it. They'd want to get rid of it, want to get better. They would be working with the doctors and their loved ones trying to keep them alive, not against them.

With anorexia, it's not you and the doctors against the disease. You and the disease are a team and your enemy is everyone else in the world. All of the people telling you that your body needs food to maintain itself. That you'll die if you stop eating. All of the people that don't worry about what they eat, they simply eat what they like or because everyone else is doing it. All of the people that love you and cry as they watch you wasting away to nothing. They're all wrong, but you and the eating disorder are right.

It sounds crazy when you say it like that. Vain even. How could everyone else be wrong? Why would they choose to lie to me? When I stood in front of Whitney [my sister] and then my friends in only my swimsuit and they described me as only bones, no, less than bones, were they lying?

They told me I was nothing. Nothing. Like I would just shrivel up and blow away in the wind. They said that my face was sunken, that my bones stuck out through my skin. They said that when they hugged me there was nothing there.

Were they lying? I don't think so. As much as I want to believe that I'm fine, that there's nothing wrong with me, I can't. Because those tears were real. The pain of those that I love is real. And I can't ignore that. I hate knowing that I'm hurting them. I hate being the cause of their tears. This realization terrifies me, because if they're right then I'm the one that must be wrong. It's not that I have a problem with being wrong. Everyone makes mistakes. Everyone can be stubborn at times. I'm stubborn a lot actually, but it's not just the being wrong part of it that scares me. It's the realization that I cannot trust myself. The realization that I cannot see things the way they really are. That the only lies present are the ones that I tell myself. My eyes lie to me when I look in the mirror or at the people around me. My brain lies when it tells me that I don't need food to survive and classifies all food and fat as bad. My vision of the world is warped and my logic twisted. I am so confused and so afraid.

MAY 23, 2009

I think we've tried everything. No, actually, that's not true. There are two last resort options that we have talked about but not done. The first is a day program at a treatment center. We've talked about this one a couple of times actually. My dietitian, Andrea, said that if I wasn't making any progress, which is their way of saying gaining weight while trying not to make me feel bad, then I'd be pulled out of school to start the day program. That was a couple of weeks ago, so I guess I must have made what they call progress. I call it failure, but I don't want to be in the day program. I think I'd just refuse if they tried to make me.

The second option is being in inpatient treatment, which basically means that I'd have to stay at the hospital until I got better. This really scares me because their idea of better is a certain weight, so what would they do at the hospital? Feed me through a tube until I reached that weight? I asked Andrea but she wouldn't tell me, so whatever it is it probably is not very pleasant.

When I first registered for outpatient treatment they said I was at a low enough weight and heart rate to be hospitalized. They actually almost didn't accept me as a patient because I was too unhealthy for them to deal with. I needed medical attention, not therapy. The only reason they allowed us to register was because they said they believed I was strong enough to fight it, and that Mom and Dad were good partners. They could take care of me together. Isn't that insane? My eating disorder was almost too strong to be taken care of at an eating disorder program. It's not just about the mental part of it anymore when your weight gets that low, because restoring your body becomes the main goal.

They all say that weight restoration is the first step in beating an eating disorder. You restore your body, get it out of the danger zone (at risk of death or organ failure), and then go through the therapy to beat the mental part of it. The part that will drag you right back to where you were before if you don't overcome it. Even if you get back to a healthy weight (what is considered a healthy weight) that doesn't always mean that your body is, or ever will be, completely restored. There can be permanent organ damage. I haven't had my period in six months. Am I going to have to someday explain to my husband that we will never be blessed with a baby because I couldn't beat my anorexia fast enough? That I was a coward and couldn't overcome my fear of food fast enough to save our potential children? I really hope not. I don't want my future husband to be added to the list of people that suffer because of my own weakness. That list seems so long sometimes.

MAY 24, 2009

I don't remember exactly when my parents first started to realize that there might be a problem. They never really said anything about my obsessive exercising, but they did notice my obsession with eating healthy. I think it annoyed them in the beginning, my constant complaining about food, but after a while they started getting worried, especially after they found out that I hadn't been getting my period.

My mom suggested that I explain the situation to Nancy, my counselor, so at our next appointment Mom left the room and I explained the situation. I told her about my obsession with exercise and the guilt I felt when I didn't have time to work out on a certain day or I didn't work out enough. I told her about my health obsessions and explained to her that I wasn't trying to lose weight. I was just trying to eat healthy.

That part of it wasn't exactly true. Maybe it started out as just wanting to be healthy, but after a while it turned into something else entirely. I was checking my weight at least once a day, and if the number didn't get lower I felt terrible. Originally, ▇lb had been my goal, my ideal weight. I exercised hard every day and started to eat less and less food depending on how hard I exercised. When I finally hit ▇lb I was thrilled, but as the number kept dropping I started to get a little worried. It didn't last long. Soon my original goal became a high number. But I didn't tell Nancy any of this.

There was one other thing I did confess though—my constant thoughts about food. That's all I thought about all day long. Food. What I would eat at my next meal. What time that meal would be at. Everything I ate was carefully planned and thought out, including the amount of exercise I would have to do to work it off.

I could tell that Nancy was very worried, but I just shrugged it off until she told me that she had to tell my mom. I got upset when she said this. I thought she had told me that everything I said was confidential, and that my parents didn't have to know unless I wanted them to. She explained that if an underage patient confessed something that was a danger to their health it became her responsibility to inform their parents.

Almost all of what I said Mom already knew, so I didn't put up too much of a fight. Then Nancy told Mom that she might want to look into an appointment with a dietitian. She brought up the eating disorder treatment center and strongly recommended it. I refused. I told them that I didn't need to see anyone, and it really wasn't that big of a deal. Yes, I had lost a large amount of weight in the last few months, but that was only because I was eating healthier. I could gain it back if I needed to. It would be easy. Exercise less or eat more, no big deal. I could take care of it.

I don't really know if I believed that or not. I still didn't really think there was a problem to take care of anyway so it didn't really matter. But the truth is, there was (is) a problem, and as much as I wanted to believe it, I couldn't fix that problem on my own. Maybe I tried. I don't remember. All I know is that my weight kept dropping. I couldn't make myself eat any more than I was (which was barely anything) and I just couldn't deal with the guilt of not exercising. I couldn't bear to watch those numbers go up.

Mom gave me a week to bring my weight up. After a couple days of losing even more weight she made up her mind. We were going to see a dietician at the treatment center. It didn't matter what I wanted anymore. I no longer had any say. I complained of course, and argued with her, but she said it didn't matter.

Our first appointment was two hours of filling out paperwork. Sheets of all my information, evaluations of how I felt, lots of bubbles to fill in. The only person we actually talked to was the lady at the front desk who gave us the papers and showed me where I could sit. The tests must have proven something because we set up an appointment to see a variety of different psychologists to analyze the situation. They all came to the same conclusion—I was (am) anorexic. I didn't, and often still don't, agree. I argued and fought but they were positive about their diagnosis.

MAY 25, 2009

I think way too much. The littlest things stress me out way more than they should. That's probably one of the reasons I have such a hard time talking to people. I keep going over different scenarios in my mind, all the little things that could go wrong. Then when I'm around people I panic. I always think they're talking about me behind my back. They think I'm annoying, stupid, ugly. These thoughts are what keep me closed in whenever I find myself around others. Honestly though, their judgment can't be anywhere near as harsh as my own judgment of myself.

MAY 26, 2009

We're doing something called the Maudsley Approach.[4] It was probably invented by some sicko child abuser that got a kick out of shoving things down children's throats while they screamed and gagged. This method of overcoming an eating disorder supposedly has one of the highest full recovery rates.

Here's how it works—I eat. All day. I can't go more than a couple of hours without eating. Just the eating part itself is a nightmare, but actually it gets worse. I don't get to choose what I eat or watch or at least have some control over how it's prepared. All I do is eat. The food gets put in front of me and I choke it down. Then a couple of hours later I do it again. And they watch me eat every bite. No hiding it, no dumping it in the sink, no giving it to one of the dogs. I am powerless. [See the notes section at the end of the book for an explanation of this treatment approach.]

* * *

When we first started meeting with Andrea, the dietician, she explained to us what happens to the body when it goes into what she referred to as starvation mode. She said that the body uses fats for energy (among other things) and once those fats are gone and it's not getting enough energy from food, it starts to use your muscle to attain that energy. So basically your body always needs something to use as fuel and if it's not given outside energy sources it starts to feed on itself. Now isn't that a lovely visualization? It also starts to shut itself down. The metabolism slows way down because the body doesn't know when it's going to be fed next.

Then you die. The end. But I never got to experience that part of it. On that note, it's time to explain what Andrea said happens to the body during weight restoration, or I guess what is happening since that's the stage I am currently in. When the body first starts getting fed again it gets uncomfortable. It has slowed everything down and suddenly there is more food than what it's used to. Then, after a while, it freaks out and realizes that it's not dying. The metabolism gets kicked into super speed and suddenly it can't be fed enough. It just wants more and more. This is because it's trying to restore itself. After this stage, once the body is restored, the metabolism stabilizes and resumes a normal speed.

MAY 27, 2009

We talked about perfectionism today in therapy and how it's good to balance out things in life. With me it's all or nothing. If I'm not going to be able to do something perfect, then I might as well not do it at all. It's that way with food. If I don't eat at all I will feel good and look good, but if I ever cave in that one bite will make me fat. For me there is no middle ground with food. Either you don't eat and feel/look good or you do eat and feel/look bad. Black and white. Good and bad. No food or too much food.

MAY 28, 2009

In seventeen months I will be eighteen years old and a legal adult. My parents will no longer have any authority. They won't be able to force me to eat. What's going to happen to me?

I thought my way of thinking would change once my body was going through restoration, but it hasn't. If anything it's gotten worse. At least before I still ate sometimes, even though it was only what I considered healthy foods. Now I don't consider any food to be healthy. Right now if my parents weren't forcing me to I wouldn't eat at all. Nothing. I don't think I could make myself do it even if I realized that I couldn't survive without it. They're the only thing that's keeping me alive. If they woke up tomorrow and decided that they weren't going to force me to eat anymore, I would probably be gone in a matter of weeks. Days maybe. I don't know how long the body can go without food. I have seventeen months to beat this thing. If I don't I will die. It's that simple.

May 30, 2009

I think I'm hungry. I can't say for sure because it's been so long since I've been truly hungry. I don't remember it being like this though. I thought hunger was felt in the stomach—a weird gurgling and bubbling. It doesn't feel like that. It feels like I'm choking. There's a strange tightness in my throat and I keep swallowing, trying to relieve it, but it doesn't go away.

I don't like being hungry. Actually I hate it. It was so much easier to not eat before. It's really uncomfortable now. My body is getting used to having food. It has started to cry out for it, but to admit hunger feels like a failure. As much as my body wants it, my mind is screaming against it. My mind is much stronger than my body.

So far I haven't told either one of my parents or my counselor (Heather) about the hunger. I don't want them to make me eat more because of it or, and I realize that this sounds slightly disturbing, to think that they are winning. The eating disorder won't go down without a fight. It's a lose-lose situation for me. Whichever choice I make will automatically be the wrong one. If I ignore the eating disorder and eat more than the bare minimum that they are making me eat, I have to deal with the constant mental abuse. I have to feel sick and bloated. To look in the mirror and be disgusted with what I see. If I can get away with less food, or only the minimal amount, it's actually not any better. I feel smug and successful at first, but then the mental torment continues. For the torment to stop the eating has to stop first. Completely.

If my parents and the people at the center get their way I end up disgusting and miserable. If the eating disorder gets its way I end up dead. Like I said before, there is really no way for me to win.

*   *   *

When the eating disorder doesn't get its way all its anger is channeled into a current of nonstop abuse. It drags me to the mirror and the blows rain down until I want to cower in the corner and hide myself from the world. It pulls my eyes to other girls when I'm in public, hissing in my head, "Look at them. *They're* skinny. *They're* good." It slips into my dreams, teaching me to fear food by not being able to control my hunger. It pushes me out of bed in the morning and keeps me in constant motion throughout the day with the threat of what the calories will do to me if I don't get rid of them. I am a slave to the monster.

I often wonder when I find myself in crowded areas if I'd somehow recognize those fallen prey to the monster. If I happened to catch their eye, would I see the beast gazing defiantly back at me? Or would I see the eyes of a soul in pain, entrapped by the confinement of their own crippled mind?

Neither I suppose. The monster is clever. If it is discovered the chances of its survival are far less. It forces its host to wear a mask so that they will appear to be fine. Then it can continue to feed on them without being recognized and without anyone hearing their screams.

A Mother's Perspective

I can still clearly remember when we took Justine to the first treatment center that specialized in eating disorders. We were sitting in a room with my husband Mat, Justine, and a few therapists and specialists. We had come for an assessment to see what would be the next step. Justine's weight was critically low. They checked her heart and her labs to determine the extent of the deterioration of her body. Her evaluation made her a candidate for inpatient treatment, a place where they could monitor her every move and, if needed, feed her with a tube. Inpatient treatment would not be a pretty thing to go through. Even the evaluators admitted it. Justine had one thing that kept an inpatient stay from becoming her reality—her mom and dad. We were a strong team. The evaluator saw something in Mat and myself that made her think that we could take care of Justine at home. She told us openly, "If I hadn't seen that you two were on the same page and willing to fight for your daughter, I would never have let her go home."

A therapist began teaching us what needed to be done. She nonchalantly made a comment about "feeding your daughter." An image of a mother with a baby in a highchair spoon-feeding her infant cereal came to mind. What the heck was this woman talking about, "feeding my daughter"? I had no idea what the next days, months, or years would entail, and I'm glad. It would have been too much to take in.

On that day we began a battle. Mat and I became a team of warriors who would spend the next few years fighting for Justine's life. We kept schedules, counted calories, learned about nutrition, and prepared her food. We watched our daughter almost every minute of the day to make sure she ate what was necessary and kept it down. We elicited the help of loved ones to supervise her eating at the rare times that we couldn't be with her.

I became obsessed with getting my daughter well. I was the driving force of the team. I devoured books on eating disorders to learn everything I could. I found myself frustrated and pained at the comments in those books because many of them, written by specialists in the field, blamed the mothers. It killed me to read those words. "Did I cause this?" I wondered. I knew in my heart that I had not. I was told by Justine that I had not, but that question would continue to haunt me.

JUNE 6, 2009

I've been questioning many things lately. Why did this happen to me? What caused it? Do all things really happen for a reason and, if so, why is this happening? What good can possibly come from it?

These questions remain unanswered, but the most important question—the one that is constantly on my mind—is no longer a mystery. I constantly ask myself, "Why am I still fighting?" It would be so much easier to just give up.

Love. That's why I keep fighting no matter how bad the pain. I love my family and friends. I can't leave them. It would hurt them too much. They cry to see me fighting, but it would rip them apart to see me give up. My sisters need me as a mentor and role model. What would that teach them if I gave up? I need to show them that trials in life can be faced and overcome. I need to be there for them when they need help. For them I will keep fighting.

My friends love me and care about me. How would they ever be able to forgive me if I left them? I can't let my own weakness, my failure, haunt them. Giving up would be so selfish. I will live with my pain if it will prevent theirs. For them I will keep fighting.

My parents are working so hard to keep me alive. Time after time I ask myself why I listen to them. They say that I have no choice and that I have to eat, but that's not true. They can't physically make me eat, so why am I doing what they say? Because I love them. If I gave up all their time and effort would have been for nothing. I can't do that to them. I can't hurt them like that. For them I will keep fighting.

Most importantly, I love my God. It is not my choice to live or to die and this is not my life to keep or throw away. It was a gift given by him. I cannot dishonor him by wasting this gift that he has given me or the blood that his son shed for me so that I could receive it. For him I will keep fighting.

June 9, 2009

Yesterday I went to Becky's school with Mom to help at her Fun and Field Day. In the afternoon I swung by the lunchroom to sit with Grace during her break. [I have three younger sisters: Whitney, Grace, and Becky.] A group of young boys at the table next to ours were yelling obnoxiously. Things like, "Who's that weird girl next to Grace?" and asking if I was married because I was wearing a ring. Naturally I ignored them. Boys that age are often extremely immature and usually the best thing to do is just to keep quiet. But later when I passed their table one of them yelled something that shocked me, "Hey, somebody said that you starved yourself."

I was surprised at how much that hurt. Who would've guessed that a comment from an oblivious little boy could make me feel so many things at once? After the shock came fear. How did they know? Were people talking about me behind my back? A few of the teachers knew. Were they faking their compassion only to turn and spread their piece of juicy gossip as soon as I had walked away? How many people in the crowded cafeteria were staring while my back was turned? In my mind, the possibilities of what they were thinking intensified my fear and embarrassment. "That's the girl that starved herself. What's wrong with her? She must be really full of herself to do something like that, or maybe she just did it for attention."

In the car I told mom what I had heard. She reluctantly admitted that Grace had asked the class to pray for me during the morning prayer petitions, and when the teacher asked why she told them. The entire class. Then, feeling guilty, she confronted her classmates one at a time and told them it was a big secret and made them promise not to tell. I guess she didn't know that telling people not to spread something is the best way to assure that it will be spread.

Grace was not trying to hurt me. I understand that now. She was only trying to help and she did not mean for the words to slip out. It's over now. What's done is done. There is no taking it back. I have forgiven her and will move on.

* * *

Something has changed. I have been feeling the hope that I thought I had lost permanently. I thought I had given up on hope.

That there was no way for me to overcome this, and even if I did survive I would be miserable forever. I wanted to be done fighting. I was sick of it, and still am, but after God opened my eyes to why I was fighting I started to feel different. To live different. To look at things differently. He gave me a new hope to replace the one I had thrown away. I have a purpose. He has a plan for my life. If I trust in him he will heal me. It may take months, maybe even years, but I will keep fighting and he will give me the strength to endure. This isn't over. This is not the end.

JUNE 11, 2009

I sunk to a new low yesterday. I just couldn't take it anymore. My parents forced the food down and I forced it right back up. By giving in to the eating disorder I've made everything much harder. Before, I ate what my parents made me eat and didn't really think there was any way around it. There was nothing I could do about it. Now there is. I know what I am capable of.

JUNE 14, 2009

Everyone sees the world differently. Not just looks at the world differently, but sees things in a unique way. Some people don't see at all. They live their life blind. They rush through life, worry constantly, and don't take the time to notice or appreciate the beauty around them. Others stop to marvel over God's creation. They are the ones that notice the little things that others miss—the intricate pattern of a flower, the delicate wings of an insect, the warmth of the sun's rays, or the smell of a summer breeze. They don't waste their time worrying about the future but live for the present moment and make every second count.

That's how I want to live my life. I want to notice and appreciate God's creation. It seems like I waste so much time worrying about the future when I should be thanking God for the gift of the present moment. He will take care of me, so I don't have to worry.

It's so much easier said than done though. I don't know how to stop the anxiety or if it's even possible. I even worry about worrying! I know that God will provide for me and my family and I say that I trust in him, but still the anxiety continues. Does that make me a hypocrite? I try not to worry or be anxious but it doesn't seem to be something that I can control.

*   *   *

I am so upset right now. I'm depressed, angry, irritated. A huge mess of bad emotions. I'm so confused, lost, broken. My life right now is a rollercoaster ride of ups and downs. The higher I climb the worse the fall.

As the day draws to a close I start to count the hours until I can curl up in a ball under the covers. It's not the sleep I crave, because I'm not actually doing much of that, it's the end of my struggle against food for that day. No more eating until morning. My contact lenses are out so I don't have to see anything in the mirror and I don't feel guilty about not moving because I'm expected to sleep and have to stay in bed. I don't sleep very much though. I toss and turn throughout the night. For the few minutes my body does drift into sleep my thoughts continue to race. My fears chase me through my dreams.

The morning brings mixed emotions. Relief from the dreams that haunt me through the night. Dread from the realization that I have to stand to burn calories as soon as possible and remain standing until I can once again curl up in bed. Depression while thinking about the day before me. And lastly, but most importantly, hope that this day will somehow be different.

A Father's Perspective

When Justine initially began writing this book, she asked me if I would be a proof-reader. I hesitantly agreed to read an early draft, mostly because I was honored that Justine asked me. I did not get very far into the manuscript. This was largely due to the flood of memories it released, most of which I had neatly tucked away never intending to dust them off and relive them again. I had to tell Justine that I would not be able to proof her book. Several months later, Justine asked if I would contribute a section to the book. This time, I figured I needed to get through it both for Justine and for myself.

It is difficult for me to remember chronologically everything that transpired during Justine's illness. This is good, I suppose, in that I don't dwell on those very difficult years. I can recall bits and pieces, some of the more memorable events, if you will. Michelle and I knew nothing about eating disorders prior to Justine's experience, but I do recall specific signs that something was not right. I distinctly recall Justine eliminating specific foods from her diet, such as butter. I also vividly remember Justine wanting to exercise excessively. Little by little, over time, we could see Justine becoming thinner and thinner.

Justine did not believe she was sick when we told her of our concerns regarding her weight loss. It wasn't until we somehow convinced our oldest daughter to stand in front of her three younger sisters in just a sports bra and shorts that something seemed to sink in. I vividly remember Whitney, Justine's stoic, next-youngest sister, breaking down in tears at the sight of her big sis reduced to skin and bones. It was startling and alarming to all of us. Something had to be done, or we were afraid we would lose our beloved Justine.

June 15, 2009

The eating disorder has a mind of its own. I don't know where its thoughts start and mine end. My mind is a mess of thoughts and emotions not entirely my own. I notice the eating disorder right when I wake up and do my morning pages (something my therapist suggested—three handwritten pages of absolutely anything that comes to mind). I am shocked by some of the things that I write about myself. Do I really feel that way? Or is it the eating disorder that's telling me how bad I am? I write very disturbing things sometimes. I write about my death, how much I hate myself, how I want to die, how it would feel. These gruesome thoughts can't be my own! Death is not going to happen until I have carried out God's plans for me. Suicide is not an option, so why do I so often find myself fantasizing about it?

*   *   *

When I first started treatment a number of the doctors asked if any part of me liked the eating disorder. I found it to be a very strange question at the time. Now I know better.

I don't like my eating disorder. I love it. It makes me stronger as a person. Other people can't lose weight because they just can't stop eating. Not me. I don't need food. I have self-control. It tells me the difference between right and wrong, good and bad. If I don't eat I will be good. Pure, self-confident, beautiful, skinny. If

I do eat I am bad. My eating disorder is also very clever. It comes up with ways of destroying food that I could never have thought up on my own. It is unjustly called a disorder. Sometimes I think of it as a guardian. A protector. There are many things I need to be protected from: food, fat, laziness, myself. Humans are weak and easily tempted. I see food as a temptation so often. My twisted mind loves the eating disorder because it keeps me from making what it categorizes as mistakes.

But then sometimes, for a brief moment, a small portion of my mind recognizes the eating disorder and sees its true form. It's a parasite and I'm the host.

June 20, 2009

When I'm angry with myself, or with my whole life or the world in general, that anger is pure pressure building up inside of me. I need an outlet because that anger is a poison that will eat at me from the inside out until the pain of it is all that I can feel.

I've never perfected a way of releasing that anger or frustration. I've tried destroying things—throwing stuff, ripping, shredding. It doesn't work. I've also tried many methods of self-harm. I've slammed up against walls and doors, punched walls, all the while desperately hoping that the physical pain will distract from the emotion.

It doesn't help much. Natasha and Sarah both cut and I've never understood why, but now I do. I've tried it a couple of times in the past when I've gotten really desperate, but my knife is dull and I've never been able to ignore the pain enough to get past that first layer of skin. I've always wondered what it would feel like to slice past that. Now I've done it. Now I know. Once again I have underestimated what I am capable of.

July 14, 2009

I am so tired. So sick of everything. Every day is just a repeat of the last. My life has no purpose, no meaning. What happened to the hope I once had? I have forgotten what joy feels like, what light looks like. Just when I think I've hit rock bottom the floor crumbles beneath my feet.

Where is my God? Has he given up on me? Left me for dead? No. He is here.

I have heard it said before that darkness and evil do not exist on their own. It is the absence of God that makes evil. The absence of light that creates darkness. Darkness is present in the areas of my life where God is not. In order to fully destroy the darkness in my life, I have to allow the light to come and replace it. Here's the hard part: How do I do that? How are my actions pushing God away from me? Basically, what am I doing wrong?

God, I know you are there. Please help me to see my mistakes and fix them. Drown out the darkness within me with your light.

July 19, 2009

I want to die. Is that wrong? I want to bleed. Is that gross? Few things are enjoyable these days. I'm tired, so tired, all the time. I try not to think about the future, but it constantly worms its way into my worries. When I think about feeling this way for days, weeks, years, an entire lifetime, I want to curl up into a ball and die. Am I going to look back at this in ten years and still feel the same? I sure hope not. Actually, I really hope that I don't make it another ten years. That's too long.

Hate is a very powerful emotion. It spreads through your mind like a weed, taking over until every cell in your body is trembling with its fire, its passion. It hardens your heart and slowly dissolves all traces of your ability to think reasonably. I have only ever hated one person: myself.

July 25, 2009

My nutritional drink [a protein shake] wants out. I can feel it gurgling in my stomach and crawling up my throat. I have the bitter taste of bile clinging to my tongue. The worst part is that I want it out too. It would be so easy. It only takes a couple of thrusts from my finger down my throat and then it's over, it's gone. This is so much harder. I've been trying to distract myself, but it's not working. Over and over I taste it on my tongue. I feel so sick, but I'm determined to keep it down.

July 26, 2009

The first time is the hardest. Like most things, the more you do it the easier it gets. I had many failed attempts before I succeeded in making myself throw up for the first time. It used to be one of those things that "other people" did. I would think about it but not too seriously. Now I think about it all the time. After every meal I look for an opportunity to lock myself in the bathroom and force the food back up.

It's funny (in a disgusting way) that of all the horrible things that can happen to your body when you make yourself throw up, decaying teeth is the only thing that sometimes prevents me from doing it.

July 28, 2009

I've been feeling like shit (excuse me) lately. The medication I was on for anxiety and then depression wasn't working so my psychiatrist switched me to a new one. Actually we're in the process of switching, which is not at all a pleasant experience. The first (and probably the hardest) part of starting a new medication is getting off the old one. This involves lowering the dosage every couple of days. It also involves terrible headaches, dizziness, and other unpleasant physical symptoms. Pam (psychologist) says that what I'm experiencing now is close to how it feels when you try to come off a drug. Oh joy. It also feels a lot like what I imagine a hangover to feel like. I promise I will never drink.

Actually, I made the symptoms a lot worse by doing something stupid. At first I did what they suggested, but then I got angry. I hate being so dependent on medication. It feels wrong, unnatural. I haven't taken anything for the last two days and it's been pure hell. The first day I just lied about it, but yesterday Mom was there watching me so I hid it under my tongue and got rid of it later. I'm worried that this will end up like my first meal plan. I'll keep hiding it until they realize it's not working and make me take an even higher dosage. I don't want that to happen. They'll find out eventually, and then I'll have to start all over. I guess I'll just take it tomorrow and plan from there. One step at a time.

AUGUST 4, 2009

I am so pissed. So so pissed. Fuck everyone. Fuck my parents. Fuck the people that call themselves my friends but don't know shit. Fuck all the shrinks that treat me like a special needs kindergartener. They say they want me to get better but they still haven't given me the chance. My parents are ordering (as if) me to start going to the eating disorder treatment center for five hours a day. No fucking way. It's not going to happen. They're making everything so much worse, and to think I actually used to get along with my parents. Those days are long gone. I hate them.

The way they see it, they are locking me up so that this monster they call an eating disorder can't get to me. The truth is they're just locking it in with me. I used to be able to feed myself. Not very well, but I could do it. Now that door is shut and locked. Instead of teaching me how to use a fork they just snatched it out of my hands and fed me themselves. Now I'll never learn and they're saying it's my fault. Assholes. Is it even possible to get any dumber?

I used to be happy, to have fun. Sure I got anxious about things, but looking at the big picture that's much easier to deal with. They kept pressing medication and I finally agreed to try it out. Now they're going nuts about how depressed I am and how nothing makes me happy anymore. When did this happen? Well, if I'm remembering correctly, it started right around the time they started force-feeding me every few hours, took away all of my privacy, and stopped letting me see my friends or do other things I liked doing because they couldn't watch or feed me. They say that my constant thoughts about food and body image are unhealthy, but how can I not think about food when I feel so gross all day long because they are constantly shoving it down my throat? How can I not think about my self-image when they constantly ask questions about it? Well I wasn't actually feeling fat, but now you won't shut up about it. They're the ones obsessing over it, not me.

AUGUST 9, 2009

Tomorrow will be my fourth day in level three (five hours every day) at the treatment center. It's Sunday today and we get weekends off, so I haven't been there since Friday.

On Tuesday night when my parents told me I would be going the next day, I thought up a whole list of things to keep me home. I was determined not to go. I took ten melatonin pills hoping that it would prevent me from waking up the next morning. Temporarily or permanently, it didn't really matter. I slept in the smallest shorts I could find and my midriff tank so that they couldn't drag me there from bed because I would be half naked. I also wrote "fuck you" in permanent marker on my stomach so that they would know how I felt about the whole thing.

My plans failed. I had figured that if I refused to go there was no way they could make me. This was not the case. I stayed in bed as long as I could and eventually they ended up physically dragging me out of bed. It was downright humiliating. After a long struggle I ended up in the car wearing shorts and a dirty t-shirt and unable to see anything because I didn't have my contact lenses in. I also had no pads or tampons and ended up having to stuff toilet paper down my pants halfway through the day (I had gotten my first period in ten months a couple of days earlier).

The day was just short of hell at worst and barely manageable at best. I couldn't see a thing and just about lost it at breakfast when I didn't know how to get the food that the dietician told me to get. I tried to explain my contactless dilemma to a dietician in the cafeteria, but my voice started cracking and I was trying not to cry so the words didn't come out right. She probably thought I was stupid, standing there with my empty tray and blubbering "I can't see" over and over. Once I got my food I found a seat in the corner and sat by myself. Nina, the only other teenager in level three that day, came over and sat by me but we didn't talk.

After breakfast we went upstairs to join the inpatient teens for "strategy" group, which so far is just going around the circle and telling how the morning has been going and how the night before went (all in regards to eating and body image, etc.). We've had this group every morning and it's always been the same thing. Level three has to go in with the inpatients because there aren't enough of us to make our own group. The meeting ended before I had a chance to say anything, so the therapist met with just the two of us afterward. Nina had no trouble talking but I said as little as possible, feeling negative about the whole experience.

Then we went to snack, which was the worst part of the entire day. I was scared and had no idea what to expect. Nina said that they'd have a sticky note with my name on it next to my snack, but they didn't the first day. There were two different snacks set out on the counter. The dietician there gave Nina hers and then told me which one was mine. It was freaking huge. Nina just had a granola bar. I had a granola bar, a protein drink, and a bowl of blueberries with some sort of white stuff on top that I assumed to be yogurt but was what the dietician labeled as a fat and turned out to be icing. It was so disgusting. I sat next to Nina but kept my head down and cried the whole time I ate.

After snack Nina and I went back upstairs with the inpatients for Medical Q & A. The first half of class was spent talking since the therapist never showed up. I talked only when asked a question but listened closely to the conversation because it was very interesting. Everyone hated being there just as much as I did, and most of them had it a lot worse off. To the inpatients who had to stay overnight, level three or four was like graduating. Most of them would have given anything to be in my position. If I remember correctly, it was at that moment that I started to feel a little better. The girls there were miserable. I thought I should really just stop complaining and be glad that I'm only there for five hours.

For the second half of class a therapist named Karen showed up. The questions were interesting, the answers even more so, but I only listened and didn't contribute to the conversation. Karen mentioned something, though, that really scared me. My parents and the dietician had been telling me that I just needed to make it to the bottom of my healthy weight range, but Karen said that the goal was to reach the middle of the range. This bothered me until I asked Pam about it. She said that it wasn't true and emailed Karen.

After Medical Q & A we went downstairs for lunch. Lunch would have been a lot worse if Karen hadn't been there. She's the teen dietician, and she helped us pick out our food and sat with us during lunch. I explained my contact situation to her and she thought it was hilarious. I tried on her glasses and found that they were close to the same prescription, so she knew what it felt like to be close to blind. I'm used to having only a cold sandwich and maybe some fruit with lunch, so the portions were overwhelming (chicken, noodles, veggies, a roll with butter, *and* cake!), but the group of girls I was with was great and Karen was really funny so she kept us entertained during the meal. After lunch we had DBT [Dialectical Behavior Therapy], which I thought was sort of weird.

That was basically it for the day. I talked to an OT therapist [Occupational Therapist] about having appointments next week and then talked to Pam for a while. I was really glad that she cleared up the information on the weight range because it was making me really nervous. I'm getting my period. I think I'm almost at the bottom of the weight range. Once I get there my meal plan goes down (hopefully by a lot).

*   *   *

Thursday went a lot better. I met Theresa (level four, first day) and apologized to Nina for being such a bitch the day before. We had some really interesting forbidden conversations while the therapists weren't around. [These were conversations having to do with our eating disorder symptoms. It is typically not helpful for people with eating disorders to talk to each other about weight or specific behaviors they engage in because it starts to be viewed as a sort of competition. I think the therapists there were also concerned that we would pick up tricks for getting rid of food, which I did.] It was really nice to be able to talk to other teens that knew what it felt like. My friends are great, but unless you've had an eating disorder you can never fully understand it.

Nina was telling us that she has this thing her mom calls her "shrine." It's a shelf in her closet filled with food that she buys at the store. Food she'd like to eat but knows she won't. Theresa used to cook for her friends and family but not eat the food she made. That's something I've done too. She has a twenty-year-old sister that tells her she's fat and needs to lose weight.

The only thing really hard on Thursday was the lunch outing. I hadn't been out to eat in a while and it was really stressful having to order (even though they told us almost exactly what to order). The lunch itself wasn't that bad. I finished my burrito fine, if not slower than most. Going to get ice cream afterwards was the hard part. I couldn't understand why no one else seemed to be having a hard time (Sam cried but ordered a flavor). I picked vanilla, which I hoped was the lowest in fat content and tried not to think about it. One of the girls got chocolate peanut butter! What the heck?!

When we got back we went to CBT [Cognitive Behavioral Therapy]. I really didn't like the therapist. She was annoying. We filled out this weird packet—my body is fat, my body is ugly, etc., etc., etc. I had a really hard time changing them into positive comments. I just used the list she gave us but didn't really believe any of them. "My body is perfect" (that was seriously one of them), yeah right.

* * *

Nina wasn't there on Friday so it was just Theresa and me. Brittany, Sam, and a "new" girl [she had been in treatment there in the past] Tammy showed up later. Theresa and I had a short and pointless argument about who was fatter. I am almost positive that I'm the largest anorexic in the building while she insists that she is. We came to the conclusion that eating disorders are really screwed up and everyone probably thinks that about themselves. (I'm still pretty sure that I'm bigger than all of the girls there, but I'm also really confused at the same time. I still don't think I can see myself.)

I don't think that the classes are going to help much or at all. The only purpose they seem to serve is to distract me between "feedings." All we do is talk about how the night before went, how today is going, or how the weekend will go. I don't understand why they think talking about it will help. I haven't had any OT (Occupational Therapy, supposed to help with body image) classes yet. I really hope those go well.

August 10, 2009

We had another FC (forbidden conversation) while the therapists weren't around. Turns out no one has much hope of ever getting rid of their eating disorder. I'm not actually sure that any of us genuinely want to. I have only been with the program for a couple of months. Some of the girls there have been in and out for years and still don't seem to be any closer to recovery.

Is this how I'm going to live my life? Constantly focused on a recovery that may never be within my reach?

September 10, 2009

I've been so up and down lately. My family believes that I'm getting better, and maybe that's what my outward appearance suggests, but I don't feel any better. I keep turning back to the same questions: Why am I doing this? What's the point? These just keep sending me on a downward spiral.

I'm doing fine in school even though I'm constantly paranoid about falling behind, but I don't really feel it. I rarely feel anything actually. It's always just blah. Yeah I get good grades, but honestly why does it matter? So I can get into what is considered a good college and then work even harder to get more good grades? Why? What's the point? So I can get into a good career? Then what? I retire at an early age and do nothing for the rest of my life? Wow, sounds like fun. I work my ass off for twenty years just so that I can work my ass off for another ten and then just stop working. Fun. Or maybe I'll have kids and all the hard work in school will be for nothing because I'll have to stay at home with them. Why am I even doing this?

September 13, 2009

I am so sick. In the brain I mean. I'm not going to the treatment center anymore because they don't think I'm getting anything out of it. That's true, but I'm not getting better like they think I am. Five months of treatment hasn't done a thing for me. I don't know what to do. I'm really stuck right now.

Some things have changed. I'm not malnourished anymore so I have more energy, and I've started to enjoy interacting with my family again. The only problem is that now they think I'm all better. Just because I'm not a walking skeleton anymore they assume my mind is healthy as well. They are so wrong. My mind is so screwed up. I've already started hiding food again. They let me eat lunch with Christian [One of my best friends in middle school and early high school. We had just started dating at the time of this entry.] because he's in on it and can watch me eat, but he can't watch me before lunch. He can't follow me to the girls' bathroom and watch me peel the cheese from my sandwich and put it in the trash. He doesn't check my lunch bag after we're done with lunch. He doesn't know that an uneaten granola bar goes in the trash almost every day.

I don't want to be sick again. It's terrible being malnourished. The constant cold. The aching body. But at the same time I don't think I want to get better either. Even when I'm supposedly not gaining weight I hate eating. The guilt is just too much. I don't always hate my body anymore. Sometimes I think that it's good just the way it is. I don't want to lose weight, but I don't want to gain either and I'm having a hard time with the concept of maintaining. It just doesn't make sense to me that my body would need that much food to maintain.

September 17, 2009

I am so tired but I can't fall asleep. Story of my life right there. I'll just keep going and going until I collapse.

I know how I would do it. I can't write it down in case I ever decide to, but I know. [I am referring to suicide here. I tried to plan it so that it would either look like an accident or no one would be able to find my body. I refer to it vaguely here so that no one would know if they found the journal after I died.]

I was excited for school at the beginning of the year, but now I'm just blah again. I feel nothing but the ever present sense of hopelessness. I think I'm going to die. I really do. My eating disorder is going to kill me. Why prolong the inevitable? I crave the food restriction like an addict craves a drug.

SEPTEMBER 19, 2009

I've been starting to think about death again. "Up the medication!" That's their battle cry in every situation. It's not helping. My parents are just wasting their money. I feel like I'm constantly fighting a current. The more I struggle, the more tired I become. Pretty soon it won't matter how hard I try. I can't fight forever. I'm tired of fighting, but I know that the second I stop the current will pull me under. If that happens I doubt that I will ever resurface.

*   *   *

I'm pretty sure that the only two journals I have ever read were *Anne Frank* and *Go Ask Alice*. They both end the same way—with an epilogue explaining their deaths. The girl in *Go Ask Alice* went through so much only to have an epilogue explaining how she killed herself.

What about my writing? Is it all for nothing? Why am I even doing this? I hope that someday my writing will inspire others in some way. Maybe someday my own journal will be published, preferably without an epilogue written by someone else.

A Mother's Perspective

In my reading, one of the statistics that I came across sent chills through my body—eating disorders are the number one cause of death among people with mental illness. I vowed that my daughter was *not* going to be one of them! I was at war with an enemy that I could not see. I was doing battle against an illness that had taken over my daughter, and I was going to win.

Sometimes the fight meant that I had to do some devious things. I had to lie and become just as deceptive as the illness had made my daughter. One of these things was to read Justine's journal. I know all about what people say related to teens being allowed to have privacy, but these were not your ordinary circumstances. I firmly believe that it was the writings in her journal that helped us save Justine. I know it was God's way of allowing us to see what we needed to do next. I would have otherwise had no idea the extent to which Justine and the eating disorder were fighting against getting well. I would never have been able to place myself one step ahead of Justine's destructive behavior to get her the help that she needed.

Every morning when Justine left the house, I would go to her bedroom to find her journal. She would usually hide it in random places and change its hiding place often. I can still remember the many times my heart would race as I searched her room. In those moments, my mind would be overcome with fear that I would be unable to find it and not know how she was doing. On the days when there had not been a new entry my heart sank. It meant that I wouldn't know what was going on in her head. On other days, I would sit reading and sob uncontrollably. The words written in that journal made my heart ache for my daughter and led me to a feeling of hopelessness that she would ever be well again.

It was then that another battle began taking place. It was a battle within me. At times when the eating disorder seemed to be gaining ground, I would feel myself sinking into despair. It hurt to watch this story unfold. It actually hurt more than anything I had ever experienced in my life. So I prayed. It was in the pain that I became closer to the Lord than I had ever been. I found myself submitting my pain, my life, and my daughter to him. Ultimately, I had to trust in him completely. It was my only choice. I could not do this on my own. It was my faith in the Lord's love for me and for my daughter that kept me fighting.

September 23, 2009

I'm almost to the end of this journal. It's weird, I remember starting it during treatment because I needed some way to sort out all of my thoughts. It's been four months since my first entry. It feels like it's been much longer. Four months isn't a very long time. It's been ten months since the end of December, the first month my eating disorder began to take control of my life.

I like to think that I was a different person then, but is that the truth? I still constantly feel fat and ugly. I'm weighed down by my guilt when I don't exercise. Am I really that different from how I was before? Even during my times of lowest weight, when I was malnourished and not thinking clearly, I would still eat a little. Not a lot, and I'd probably feel guilty after, but I'd still do it. But now I don't think I could. If my parents weren't around I would just stop completely even though I'd subconsciously know what would happen.

September 25, 2009

I am so sick of living like this. All I ever feel is guilt. Nothing is ever good enough. I am so far from being the person I want to be.

September 29, 2009

You'd think that not eating would save you a lot of time. No snacks, so you don't get interrupted during study time to go to the fridge. No breakfast, so instead of taking time to make something you can use that extra time to get ready for school. No lunch, so you don't have to drop everything you're doing and spend extra money on fat. No dinner, so you can stay out late without being interrupted. Plus without all that food you're looking better and better.

Actually, it doesn't work that way. It's like skipping sleep. First you are tired, but after that passes you start to feel awake again! Eventually though, with your body missing out on sleep it's all you can think about. Your eyes start to feel heavy and you stop paying attention to external factors because all you can think about is how tired you are.

Having an eating disorder is an obsession. It becomes your life. As your body begins to shut down, over and over again it turns to the one thing you need—food. When you're not eating you're thinking about it.

"I'm so hungry. No, maybe I'm not hungry. I can't tell. I ate a big breakfast so I don't need lunch. I feel so guilty. I shouldn't have eaten that."

It doesn't get any better when you do eat. Those thoughts are still there.

"I can't believe I'm eating this. I am so fat. I shouldn't be eating this. Am I really hungry? I'd better leave a little on my plate. Maybe they won't notice if I slip some under my napkin. Maybe after I can get rid of it. It's too much food. I shouldn't be eating this much. They're not eating this much. Wow, look at how much they're eating. They're so lucky that they can eat and still stay thin. I wish I could do that."

Your eating disorder becomes a career, a hobby, your lover, your life. There is no time for anything else. When you're at school you're constantly comparing body types instead of paying attention.

"Ha, look at how fat she is. I'm so glad that I'm not that fat. If I were it would be easy to lose weight. Other people can't do it, but I can. Look at how skinny she is. She is so lucky. I wish I could be that skinny. I am so fat."

When you're not comparing you're plotting, thinking of your next meal and how much you're going to eat (or not eat). Thinking about the type of exercise you'll do that day.

"I don't want to eat too big of a lunch because that will make me fat, but if I don't eat lunch at all my metabolism will slow down and that will also make me fat. I have so much homework tonight. When am I going to work out? I need to work out. We're having pizza tonight for dinner. I can't sit or stop moving. If I do I won't be burning calories. I'll just go through the workout tape right before I do my schoolwork. I can do it fast, and it will keep my mind off the after-school snack that my sisters are having."

If I'm so in love with my eating disorder, how can I love anyone else? The relationship I have with my eating disorder is made up of lies. I can never be completely honest with a person while I'm hiding so much from them. "I feel sick." A lie. "I already ate." A lie. "I don't like this. I can't eat in front of people. I'm not hungry." They're all lies. When I hide food, throw up, exercise when I'm not allowed, I'm lying. My eating disorder can't handle the truth though, so for now I'll have to just keep lying.

September 30, 2009

I weighed myself yesterday. I haven't known my weight in months. That's one of the first things they did—take the scale away. It took me a while to find it, but I knew it was somewhere in Mom's room because it magically appears from there whenever she needs to weigh me. It was wrapped in a pair of her old jeans on the bottom of the shelf. Clever, but obviously not clever enough. I was terrified when I stepped on. I was guessing that I'd weigh about ▮▮ lb. I wasn't even close. I only weigh ▮▮ lb. What a relief.

October 2, 2009

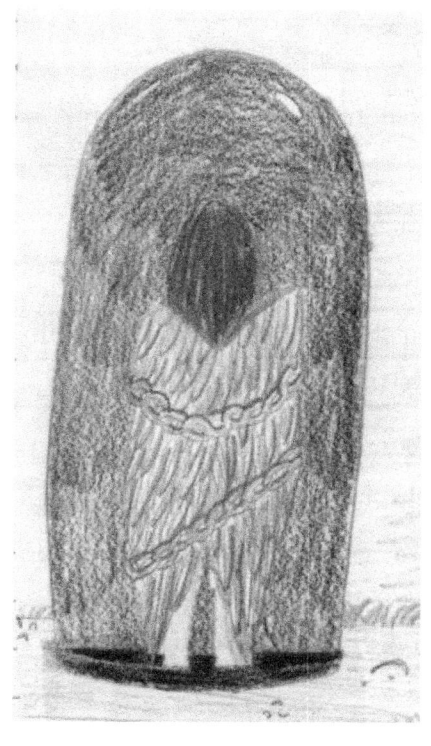

A couple months ago in art therapy we had to draw pictures of our eating disorder. Here is mine:

I may have once had potential but not anymore. I am bound by chains, confined within the darkness of my own mind. There may be hope, but if there is I don't see it.

I am so tired, so sick of everything. All I do is homework, read, homework, read, homework, read. Books are my only relief. I absorb myself in them the best I can so that they will take me away from the never-ending stream of anxious thoughts. What is my motivation? I try not to think about it. Thinking about the future just depresses me. I take one book at a time, one homework assignment at a time. That's all I have. I don't know why, I just do. Do do do. Like eating. I already hate eating, and I constantly crave the relief that death would bring, so why do I do it?

October 4, 2009

My birthday is coming up. I don't know what to think. Last year on my birthday Christian and Jenny both brought me chocolate at school. I don't remember if I ate it or not. When Dad's side of the family came over a couple of weekends ago to celebrate birthdays, as I blew out the candles my wish was that I wouldn't have to eat the cake. My wish came true. Yay. Happy birthday to me.

Seventeen is just one year closer to eighteen. Eighteen, when I'm a legal adult. I won't have to listen to my parents anymore. Will they still be able to make me eat? My eating disorder is overjoyed. I'm terrified.

* * *

I've been losing weight. My parents found out about me hiding food. Shit. They said I have to go back to the treatment center. I hate it there. If I get taken out of school and put into inpatient or partial it's over. I'm done. I will not let them wreck my life. I'm staying in school. That's all there is to it.

My heartburn is getting worse and worse. Mom thinks I might have damaged something by throwing up. She thinks I'm still doing it, which makes me wish I were, but I'm not. I hate this. I wish I could just vanish off the face of the earth.

October 10, 2009

Christian is coming over in a little bit. I have a killer headache and I'm so tired. I've lost almost all of my motivation. I can't concentrate. My schoolwork seems so pointless. I don't talk to any of my girlfriends anymore. On Wednesday I cried for the first time in a long time. I couldn't stop. I just kept crying and crying and crying. I laid in bed and texted a bunch of people because I was so lonely. No one texted back. They probably have a ton of stuff going on.

October 12, 2009

Tonight in my study skills class we were assigned to work in groups. This really pretty girl sat in front of me. She wore no makeup but was still beautiful. I've often admired her hair from the back of the class where I sit. Until I was sitting directly across from her, I'd never noticed the pink scar on her neck. It may have been some sort of accident, but that's not what it looked like. I know what self-harm scars look like. I have them all over my stomach. I'm pretty sure her scars were from an attempted suicide (I know that might not be true, but it still got me thinking). My first thought was a disturbing one. Why on her neck where it would be completely obvious if she failed? Why not her wrists? I imagined myself approaching her and telling her that it was dumb to try to cut her neck. That she should have thought of another, less painful way. Why hadn't she used a gun or car exhaust?

At that moment, something in my brain clicked into place and I was faced with the startling realization of my cruel thoughts. Up until recent months, if someone would have asked me if suicide were okay I'd have said no. Now when I see people with their battle scars I feel connected. Instead of the shock and horror I would have shown a few months back, I find myself approving of their actions and in some cases wanted to offer advice. Natasha doesn't know that I cut, but if she did I would have called the moment I discovered razor blades and made sure she's not still using a paperclip. If I drank I would probably have called Sarah to make sure she knows what the best brands are and what the best time is to get drunk. When I see overweight people I think about all the things I could teach them. "It's so easy. All you have to do is just not eat."

It's strange how I still constantly want to help people. But really, I am helping no one now. If I had told the girl in class what I had been thinking, would I really have been helping her or would I have been killing her? If she listened to my advice and was successful, would her blood be on my hands? Not that it really matters. What matters is that if I really want to help people I'm going to have to make a change. One person can make such a huge difference. Her scar is not a sign of failure but of courage. Death is easy. Life is not.

We will, eventually, get to spend eternity with our Father in heaven. Is it not worth the pain of a single lifetime if my actions will lead others to him? Yes it's hard, yes it hurts, but this pain won't last forever. If my presence will bring even a little bit of joy to others, then every moment of my pain will be worth it.

I have not given up. This battle is not over. God has a plan for my life and I will give everything I have to accomplish it. Jesus, I love you. Jesus, I trust in you. This is not over.

October 17, 2009

Christian and I were watching a movie last night and the main character said something that really touched me. He was praying for his girlfriend and he asked God to send someone that would make her happy. Not that she would be with him, but that she would be happy.

My prayer is very similar. God, I care so much about Christian. All I want is for him to be happy. He deserves to be happy. I don't want my depression to wear off on him. I don't want my disease to kill him also. God, if this is going to end badly please undo his connection to me. Send him a girl that will love him unconditionally, not one that is already married to an eating disorder.

Sometimes I wish that I'd never met him. Then I would be just another dying human. Now I'm afraid that if I die I will take part of him with me. I can't do that to him. I can't kill him. If I had one wish, I'd wish that all the people who know and love me now would have never met me. I'm causing them pain, and I hate myself for it. Whitney, Grace, Becky, my parents, my friends, Christian. I'm hurting them, but I don't know how to stop. Dying would end my pain but not theirs.

October 22, 2009

Lately, I have found myself drifting further and further away from my friends. I'm pretty sure that means that my depression is getting worse. That's what I've heard anyway.

I listened to a talk at my school about bipolar disorder and did a free screening for depression and anxiety. I was high for both. The guy who looked over my paper seemed a little bit worried. I just told him that I was there for the extra credit so I could leave.

Today in psychology class, when the teacher asked us to write down the most satisfying moment of our week all I could think of was sleep. Sad. Luckily we didn't have to turn the papers in. I feel tired all the time, and then I feel guilty because I'm eating and not exercising.

October 24, 2009

What's happening to me? I don't even feel like writing anymore. I'm always so tired. For a while I would never let myself sit down. Now I'm sitting or lying down most of the day. I have no muscle. My legs burn just from walking up the stairs. It's getting even harder to do my schoolwork. I have a final exam, presentation, and paper due in my study skills class that I haven't even started working on.

October 28, 2009

In my study skills class we learned that one of the key factors of motivation is having a goal to work towards. I have always had academic goals but rarely do I have personal ones. Last night I decided that the best way to fight my steadily growing depression is with goals. Perhaps they will help the meaning return to my life. Each day I'm going to make a list (three or so) of personal goals to achieve. I'll start off small, and then work my way towards larger goals.

Last night I had to write myself a note because I was worried that I wouldn't feel like doing it in the morning. It says, "I don't care if you feel like it or not; you're doing it." Well this morning, and just as I suspected, I feel unmotivated to get motivated. But here I am anyways writing my goals.

Today I'm going to smile at three strangers. This wouldn't be a big deal for normal people, but I am obviously not normal and it will be hard for me. Just to clarify—not a full out teeth smile, just a lips and eyes smile. Maybe, with this small act, I will be able to make someone happy. Eventually, I want to be able to greet people and give compliments to strangers (something I'm uncomfortable doing now).

* * *

I did it. I smiled at three random people today. It was a lot harder than I thought it would be. I realized today that I have a hard time even making eye contact. When I walk I automatically look at the ground. The first person was a little bit awkward. He didn't look up until the last second before I passed him and I'd already been smiling at him. He probably thought I was crazy. The second and third were almost natural. At the thrift store I held a door open for a mother with a baby and she thanked me. I didn't even have to think about smiling to make it happen. Then, at school, a man was coming up the stairs and we both smiled. It's funny to think that most people aren't aware that they smile. Maybe it was just because of my set goal, but I noticed every smile today.

* * *

Only a couple pages left of my journal. Grandma gave me a new one for my birthday and I'm excited to write in it. I hate leaving things unfinished. Maybe if I always have a journal to write in I'll choose to live because I don't want to leave it unfinished. Seems like a good plan.

OCTOBER 29, 2009

Today I'm going to (1) pick up something of someone else's without being asked (dishes might be good. I could wash them while Mom is not around), (2) be really careful about what I say (be careful not to snap at anyone), and (3) give a hug to someone other than my parents or Christian.

I got all of these done. I washed Grace and Becky's dishes and gave Becky a hug. I didn't yell at anyone, but I'm going to have to work harder with not snapping.

NOVEMBER 1, 2009

The other night I had a dream that I was malnourished again. I kept trying to stand but my legs wouldn't support me. Each time I stood I fell over.

I start working at the gift shop tomorrow. My first job (besides doing inventory for them). I hope the manager will allow me to wear my nose ring. That would suck if I had to take it out. I also have my first appointment with my new eating disorder shrink. That should be tons of fun.

NOVEMBER 2, 2009

It's strange how nonstereotypical my relationship with Christian is. I'd always heard that it's the guys you have to worry about. They're the ones that are scared of commitment. In our relationship that's me. I don't want to bond with people. I want to live by myself without anyone worrying about me. Then I can eat when I want to and, eventually, curl up and die alone. That's what I want.

November 9, 2009

I found a new and completely disgusting game to play. I've had problems with my vision going black for a while, but never to the extent that I'm experiencing now. Last week I stood up after stretching and ended up falling over. Not only do I see a black haze but I also experience a brief shaking sensation (I don't know if my body is physically shaking).

Anyway, the other day I discovered the best way to bring about these fade-outs. It seems like they keep getting more intense each time they happen. I've done it multiple times today. The last two times I experienced a short memory loss. I stand and arch my back, raising my hands over my head. Then the darkness comes (just as I'm about to give up hope that it will) and I try to stand but I usually end up slouched against the wall shaking. When I snap out of it, it feels like waking from a dream. It seems like I experienced the whole thing and should remember it, but for a few seconds it's gone from my mind.

* * *

We went to see that terrible, stereotypical counselor today. Just thinking about it upsets me. She was so detached from the whole thing. She didn't seem to care about what was going on. She just wanted to sound like she knew what she was talking about. Oh, and she also drives me crazy. Did I mention that? I was so pissed when we left the office. I sat in the back of the van and refused to comment on anything Mom said.

NOVEMBER 14, 2009

"God grant me the grace to accept with serenity the things that cannot be changed, courage to change the things that can, and the wisdom to distinguish them."

I've read this three times this week. The first time was on a plaque at the gift shop, the second was in one of Mom's eating disorder books, and the third was in my psychology textbook (I didn't really notice until I read it in my psychology book. That was a little strange).

At mass tonight I saw the truth. When it comes right down to it there are only two choices: my eating disorder or my God. I cannot serve both. I need to change. God give me the courage to change!

November 26, 2009

I lost it today during mass. I felt emotional pain, and then felt the urge stronger than I ever had before. I wanted to bleed. Needed to bleed. I clawed at my wrist when my sisters weren't looking and, when that didn't work, scraped it against the zipper of my coat. Still nothing. I went to the bathroom to check the paper towel dispenser, but the jagged edge was located on the inside of the machine. I locked myself in a stall and scraped my wrist against all the metal I could find, but none of it was sharp enough. Then I used my teeth. I pressed all the way to the bone, leaving red and blue teeth marks but no blood.

When I got home I took a pin from the billboard in my room and punctured my wrist. Twice I broke through skin and tried not to cry out as the needle slid inside. I still don't understand why the needle didn't draw blood. I know for a fact that it went through the skin.

Finally, I grabbed the one thing that I was certain would work: my razorblade. Wrists show so I could only do a small cut, but it felt amazing. It was like the pressure inside of me built up until I was in danger of exploding. Then I let that pressure trickle out through my cut.

December 7, 2009

I haven't felt like writing lately. Actually I haven't felt like doing anything. I'm depressed because my homework is done. It doesn't get any more pathetic than that. I don't like having free time. I want to go go go, never stop to think. When my head is empty the eating disorder sneaks in to tell me how worthless I am. I hear Ed every moment I'm not doing something productive. [This was the name I gave to the eating disorder. A therapist suggested I do this in order to separate myself from the illness. This made it easier for both my family and I to distinguish which thoughts were truly mine and which belonged to the disease.]

"You're so ugly. I don't understand why someone as good looking as Christian would ever consider you dateable."

"Damn, feel that stomach. Could you get any fatter? How many rolls is that now, twenty?"

"I can't believe you're actually eating that without a fight. Do you have any idea how fattening Twinkies are?"

"I love you like a fat kid loves Twinkies. Oh look you are a fat girl eating Twinkies! What a coincidence."

"You never even tried. Most girls stick with me for years. You're going to leave me after a couple of months?"

I could probably fill this entire book with the nasty comments that Ed throws at me. Even now I'm aware of my hanging stomach, flabby boobs and arms, and the fact that my fat ass is not moving/burning calories because I am sitting.

Supposedly I'm dropping weight again. If I continue to drop my parents will make me go to the day program as soon as Christmas break starts.

December 19, 2009

I'm over my extreme childhood fears. I watched some horror movie trailers last night. I'm not sure why that sort of stuff doesn't bother me anymore. I think I'm probably too afraid of food to acknowledge any of my previous fears. My nightmares are about losing control and eating without someone telling me to. There is nothing that scares me more than this.

December 23, 2009

I told Christian everything. He knows that I cut, he knows I'm depressed, and he knows that I don't think I'll be alive for very long. He didn't break up with me. He visited me at work yesterday and called me this morning to talk and see if I wanted to hang out this afternoon. Either he really does love me or he's doing it out of pity. I don't want his pity. I wish I could know for certain if he hangs out with me because he likes spending time with me or because he feels responsible for me somehow. I don't like feeling so vulnerable. I don't want him to know how much I adore him or how many times I've pictured a bullet and then seen his face instead.

December 24, 2009

I wonder how many times I've started entries with the words "I'm so depressed." Not this time I guess. I feel terrible. This morning was good, but now Dad's family is over and I don't feel well. I want to go to bed. We're going to mass at eleven tonight, so I won't be able to get in bed for at least seven hours.

Christmas is tomorrow. Yay. I just want to curl up and sleep right now, but that's not an option. I'm getting tired of reading all the time. There goes the last thing that could keep the thoughts away.

December 25, 2009

Today went pretty well. Dad liked the game I got him a lot. It is actually pretty neat. It was weird not going up to Grandpa's but kind of nice to be able to hang out in our pajamas.

I am the most depressed when I'm not doing something productive. This morning it was great to watch everyone open gifts and to have the chance to experience some family bonding time. After breakfast it started going downhill. I loaded all the songs I could find on my new MP3 player, and then with nothing to do I began to feel tired yet again.

I hope everyone had a great Christmas. They seemed really happy today.

December 30, 2009

Once again my parents are threatening me with the day program. I have two appointments this Monday to see what the treatment team thinks about my situation. I can't imagine them not wanting me to come in more. They're the ones getting paid.

I'm starting to really want to beat this eating disorder. It's destroying my life and the lives of those close to me. Sometimes I really do feel that I can overcome this. Then I remember the weight gain and am quickly consumed by doubt. I want so badly to be beautiful, to be thin. The worst part is how easy it is not to eat. It is rarely uncomfortable for me anymore.

December 31, 2009

I am so sick of this! I want to get better. I do. I do. I do. I can't say that I'll want that tomorrow or in the next hour, but right at this very moment I want to get better. I miss my friends. I miss my old life. I don't miss looking in the mirror and hating what I see. I miss looking in the mirror and not caring what I see. This is my body. God meant for me to have curves.

The scary thing about trying is that you can fail. When you don't try you can't fail. What if I try and find that I can't change? That's what I'm afraid of.

January 14, 2010

It's been about a week since I last cut. Today when I went to grab Sophie [my pet rabbit] from the floor she scratched my wrist and the urge returned. The stinging felt so good. I didn't want to cut for all the wrong reasons (too long of a process, hard to clean). I ended up not cutting myself after all, but the alternative was not much better. For the second time I used the lighter instead. A burn feels so good, but the pain only lasts for a while.

Feeling very frustrated and in need of someone else to confide in, I went onto an online ministry site I'd heard about on the radio. They had a live chat where you could ask questions. The first person I talked to thought self-harm was wrong but wasn't very convincing about it. After a couple of minutes she switched me over to someone else. He seemed to know exactly what to say. When I asked him what God thought about self-harm he asked me what any father would think if his child was harming themselves. He gave me a verse:

"For you have been purchased at a price. Therefore, glorify God in your body." [New American Bible, 1 Corinthians 6:20]

He said that my body belongs to God. When I mentioned the eating disorder and how I'm supposedly just not eating because I don't like food and think I eat enough already, he said that if my doctor says it's not good for my body then I was "not being a wise caretaker of the Lord's property."

January 22, 2010

I'm completely off my medication (for depression, not for sleep). I don't really feel much different. I never do. The medication just doesn't seem to affect me.

I can hear the rain hitting my window. It will most likely snow tomorrow, but for now it's rain. I like it. The sound is very calming. I'm so tired, and my bed feels so good. I want to curl up under the blanket and sleep forever.

January 23, 2010

I am the ugliest bitch ever. I hate mirrors. I was so tired today. I'm not sure if the exhaustion was mental, physical, or a combination of both. I don't feel like writing anymore.

January 24, 2010

This isn't going to work. I can't live my life like this. Last week I threw away my blades. I hate not having them. The other day I went to retrieve them and found my hiding places empty. I miss them. Without them I have no release, no way to escape the pain. All I can do is curl up into a ball and wait for the numbness to once again make me mobile.

I'm not sure how much longer I can physically endure this. I haven't yet reached the level of depression that would keep me from getting out of bed, but judging by my constant exhaustion I can't be that far away.

God, I need you. I've always needed you. Please give me the strength to get up each morning.

FEBRUARY 16, 2010

I haven't written anything lately. I haven't felt like it. I haven't felt like doing much of anything. I do my homework. That's it. Grace commented on how much homework I'm always doing the other day. She says that she doesn't want to do college classes while in high school because it looks like too much work. There's much less work than what I make it look like. I'm just trying to stay busy. What would I do with free time? I have no passion, no hobbies. I focus on what I have to do and try my best to ignore that fact. Like most of my thoughts these days it's depressing.

FEBRUARY 22, 2010

Today was my first day on a new medication.

MARCH 23, 2010

Last night I had a dream that Christian had a stroke and was in the hospital dying. I woke up crying and nauseous. I literally felt sick and was worried that I would throw up. I spent the rest of the night thinking about how I would kill myself if he died. If I could get a gun (which isn't very likely because my parents would probably guess at what I wanted to do with it), I'd just shoot myself in the head. Quick and foolproof. I wouldn't be able to find meaning in my life if he were gone.

MARCH 27, 2010

I told Christian about my dream and he said that he reacted the same way when I told him that I thought I would die early and I didn't really want to live anyway. He said that he wouldn't want to live either if I died. I found that surprising but could tell that he meant it. Why though? It doesn't make any sense. He has a passion and love for life that I don't have. He has dreams and a future. I have nothing. A part of me hates him for keeping me alive. He has so much and I can't risk wrecking that.

MARCH 28, 2010

I think I'm going to go to a college close to home. I'd like to be able to live at home and just drive up to school during the day like I'm doing now. I'm not sure that I could live on my own. There are a couple of reasons for this choice.

First of all, I'd like to stay with my family. I want to be there for Grace and Becky's childhood. Marissa, Anne, and Sarah never get to see their older siblings and they really miss them. I want to make an effort to be an active part of my sisters' lives. I'll have to work extra hard to earn my keep. I don't want my parents to think that I'm mooching off of them. Living at home will also save a lot of money. I won't have to pay for a dorm and if I keep driving my sisters around Mom and Dad will probably pay for my gas.

The third reason is that I'm not sure that I could live on my own. It's been more than a year that my parents have had to give me every bite of food that I eat. I still hate the way I look and hide my food every chance I get. I don't think that I could make myself eat if I were alone.

April 18, 2010

I feel dirty all the time. Even right after I get out of the shower I feel fat and sweaty and gross. I don't like wearing nice clothes when I feel like this. It seems like I'll wreck them. Also, I don't want it to look like I'm trying too hard. I feel like big, grimy T-shirts and sweatpants are perfect for me. Then everyone will know that I know what I look like. There's no point in pretending that I'm something I'm not.

May 28, 2010

I want to write something but I don't know what. All of my fiction seems pointless. I want to help people but I don't know how to do that through my words.

June 16, 2010

I feel like I need to update since I haven't written in a while. I started cutting again. I went without it for a while before caving in. I had an argument with Grace and that pushed me over the edge. I don't even remember what it was about, that's how insignificant it was, but I remember the feelings of anger and frustration that brought my thoughts back to the blade. I didn't put up much of a fight. The urge rose and suddenly that was all I could think about. I needed to cut. Needed it. And at that exact moment too.

I don't feel much regret about it. Once I've finished cutting I'm not left with the feelings of intense shame and discouragement that I walk away with after participating in other types of sin. Does that mean that it's not as bad? I'm not hurting anyone but myself. I'm sure it makes God sad (which, now that I think about it, should really be enough to make me stop), but I don't think that it affects our relationship or changes the way I see other people. I guess I really don't know. I'll have to pray about it.

June 25, 2010

After mass we went to a restaurant called My Sister's Place. I really hate eating at restaurants. Everything I've read seems to suggest that food in restaurants is ten times worse for you than anything you'd make at home. I ended up getting a salad with grilled chicken and it was enormous. While I waited for Whitney to finish up in the bathroom so I could take my turn, I studied the picture display on the back of the bathroom door. It was covered with photographs of sisters who had eaten there. A plaque on the wall alongside the display caught my eye (more specifically, the words "eating disorder" on it caught my eye). It was a memorial to the three sisters in the picture, one of which had "lost a battle against anorexia after a long struggle" and died. I showed it to Whitney and she said either "That could be us" or "That's going to be us." I don't remember which, though I wish I did since they obviously imply very different things.

Later, Mom got up to go to the bathroom and I braced myself for the explosion I knew would happen. It did. She fled from the restaurant in tears. I don't understand this disease. Both Whitney and Mom's reactions left me feeling ashamed but also smug. Where did that come from? I hate hate *hate* that I'm hurting the people that I love, but at the same time I feel almost prideful of my eating disorder. It doesn't make any sense.

July 6, 2010

This is it—the beginning of the end. The end of the eating disorder. With God's help I was able to take the first step. I had a long talk with Mom about what was keeping me from turning the eating disorder over to God. All of the reasons were superficial, lies actually. The worldly/false knowledge that comes with it is so seductive. Seeing my flaws and the flaws of the people around me seems like a gift at times, but it's not and the flaws that I see are not real.

Mom and I drove up to church and for the first time I asked God to free me from the eating disorder. Never before have I been able to say with sincerity: I *want* to get better. Now I can.

I want to get better. The journey won't be easy. It's going to be long and painful, every day a new battle, but I know that if I continue to reach out to God he will be with me every step of the way.

July 8, 2010

The eating disorder changes the way I see people. The more in tune I am with God, the easier it is for me to see not only the outward beauty of people but the inward beauty as well. The eating disorder hides all that. With its eyes I only see their flaws and cannot get past to what's underneath.

July 11, 2010

I threw away my blades this morning. Today is my ninth day clean (no throwing up, lying about food, getting rid of food). I've still been complaining about portions a little bit and trying to eat less when I can. I realize that behavior will have to go eventually, but for now I'm not counting that as a win for the eating disorder. Basically, it's been nine days since I made the choice to change with God's help and nine days since I've let the eating disorder result in any extreme behavior.

It's getting harder. It seems like the last few days I've been extra aware of my stomach and thighs. Every time I move I can feel them pressing against my clothes and it's driving me crazy. The exercise compulsions are worse too and I hate hate hate them. The guilt has been pounding at my head all day for the last few days.

My own addictions follow the pattern of others. It seems almost easy at first. Like I could just choose when to stop and, bam, no more eating disorder, no more cutting. After a few days it starts to get harder. The cravings pop up unexpectedly and the guilt sneaks in faster than you're aware of it. Then there's that voice, sweet with suggestion—

"Just one tiny cut. You'd feel so much better" or "You're healthy now, but that piece of cheese might put you past the healthy mark and nearing fat. Just slip it off. No one will notice."

The only problem is, you give into the suggestion just once and it's back to square one. The addiction doesn't have to rebuild itself. It continues right where it left off.

I've tried a couple times to quit cutting and then gave in and started all over again. So far I've stayed clean eating disorder wise, but it hasn't been long. Honestly though, how much time has passed doesn't really matter. Many people (don't want to say most, sounds pessimistic) relapse even years later. The effects will be the same—back to square one (at least that's what I've read and heard, and it may be dangerous to convince myself of anything different. I don't recall reading anything specific about how ED relapses usually work so I can't say for sure that it would be the same as other addiction, but it sure seems like it would be).

July 25, 2010

Things are happening so fast. Twenty-two days clean today. I'm still counting not lying or throwing anything away as clean. I still hear the voice of the eating disorder constantly. Today I went grocery shopping for Mom. I had to grab two boxes of cereal bars for my lunches. The eating disorder made me check the labels of each type to see if any were better than the others. Apparently raspberry cereal bars have ten more calories than the other fruit types. Guess which type I picked (hint: not raspberry). The eating disorder tells me that I'm fat, ugly, and worthless still too. The fat and ugly I have a hard time not agreeing with, but I know I'm not worthless. Would Christ have suffered and died for someone he viewed as worthless? No way! I try not to dwell too much on my weight or the way I look. It's not too hard when I keep my sights focused on God. Then those things seem insignificant (as they should be).

* * *

I've been experiencing a large amount of anxiety about my vocation lately. The path is unclear to me right now. I don't know if I'm called to be married, single, or something else. It doesn't seem like I'd be able to do the intense counseling work I want to do and still have time to raise a family. For a while this question kept bothering me: Does God want me to get married and have children or live a single life and focus on work? Am I going to live for my work or my family? God gave me the answer to that last one: neither. I am going to be living for him. That is the only part of my calling that I need to worry about. If I live first for him, his plans will fall into place. I know this to be true, but can't seem to stop the anxieties sometimes anyway.

I brought the whole vocation thing up with Christian last night. It wasn't a great night for rational conversation though at first. The anxieties had built up over the last few days (if we should be dating, I must not be called to marry him because he wants to have kids and I'm not sure that I'll be able to physically or with a job, etc., etc., etc...) and I was pretty much a wreck. My plan had been to bring up the stuff I was worrying about, but I ended up having a little anxiety/depression attack. I told him I had to use the bathroom and then locked myself in there and cried. Nice.

He's positive that he is called to be married but not necessarily to have children. He'd love to have kids of course, but he's ready to also accept it if that is not God's will for him. I don't know God's plan for the future, but we both (Christian and I) agree that right now we are exactly where we're supposed to be. Christian said that he's prayed a lot about our relationship and he strongly believes that if something was wrong about it he would know. He also said that love is not just a feeling, it's a commitment. Then he said that he loves me. That's something that he's absolutely positive about.

July 31, 2010

Some irony: because I was so quiet in class, during the first seventh grade parent-teacher conference my homeroom teacher told my parents that she was worried about me. She thought I might be depressed. We laughed about it when we got home but months later depression hit hard. When I first started at my high school, Mr. Anderson told Mom that he was worried about me because he never saw me eat at school (I had lunch at home). We laughed about that too. "Haha, he thinks I have an eating disorder or something." Hmm...

August 10, 2010

Today while I was driving Whitney to Janine's house she told me about a dream she had the night before. She was having a piano concert and was really excited to see us (the family). Mom,

Dad, Grace, and Becky came, but she was wondering where I was. Minutes later, I was rolled into the room in a hospital bed. I was dying because of the eating disorder. She said that she had a hard time playing then because she was so upset. She kept having to stop to compose herself.

August 12, 2010

While I was cleaning out the cabinets for Mom today, I came across the worst photo I have ever seen of myself. It was from August of 2008, only two years ago, and I was so fat. It was disgusting. I actually had a chest, but my stomach was the same size. It was pretty much bulging out of my shirt. It actually made me glad to have an eating disorder. There is so much more I want to say, but I am so tired.

August 22, 2010

I cheated today. Kind of. I put one piece of chicken on my sandwich instead of two like I usually have. It wasn't really a weight thing though. There was just one piece of chicken left and I didn't want to open a new bag. It's been over a month since I've done anything like that. Do I have to start over? Maybe I'll just not count days. Ugh, I don't know. It honestly wasn't an eating disorder thing, but that doesn't mean that the eating disorder wasn't happy about it. And it was lying because my parents expect me to put two pieces on.

August 23, 2010

Crap crap crap. I didn't put butter on one of my pieces of toast this morning. I want to say it wasn't eating disorder related, but what the heck do I know anyway? Sometimes I still don't even think I have an eating disorder.

September 12, 2010

I can feel the depression creeping up on me. I've had a really good couple of weeks, but I can feel myself sliding. People have proven that depression is an actual, physical disease in the brain, but often I feel like it's my fault. Like I'm not trying hard enough to be happy or praying enough or something. I feel like if I'm really filled with the Holy Spirit I should be happy all the time.

Dad was reading this booklet on Mother Teresa and he said that during her lifetime she did not feel God's presence very often. Mostly she felt darkness. And yet she was such a holy woman, filled with so much love.

I don't understand the way God works and I probably never will. Sometimes I feel his peace or remarkable joy (like a taste of heaven), but other times I feel such darkness. Ah, even now just thinking about these moments of joy makes me smile. Someday when I am living in paradise I will probably be able to know the reason for darkness if I want to. But in God's holy presence and in the midst of so much joy I really doubt that I'll care.

September 29, 2010

I'm not doing very well. I had an especially bad day today. I haven't been putting on mayonnaise or butter when I'm not being watched and sometimes I pour skim instead of one percent milk. Today I switched my glass with Becky's when no one was looking so I could have skim milk. Then when Dad went upstairs to get ready for hockey I put some of my hamburger and bun in my pocket. It was gross and I felt horrible.

October 3, 2010

I lost weight. I am now ▮▮lb. That's only 11 pounds away from the smallest I've ever been when they wanted to put me in the hospital. Mom is so upset. She blew up at me a couple days ago when I wasn't going to eat my potatoes. She was screaming and crying. She said "You're killing us!"

Us? Who's us? I felt/feel so horrible. Why can't I just deal with this thing? I hate that it hurts the people I love. I want to want to get better, but I still don't always want to (if that makes any sense). I guess I know who us is. I'm not just killing myself. I'm killing those that love me also.

* * *

It's almost my birthday. I'm excited, but also a little afraid. Christian says that because I'm living with my parents nothing really changes. I'm not so sure about that. Mom was threatening to send me back to the treatment center a couple days ago. Can they do that if I'm 18? I keep telling the eating disorder that they can't as a way to temporarily stall it. I tell it that I can't lose weight right now, but in a couple of weeks I'll be able to do whatever I want. I don't know if that's actually true, but I have no other excuses and I'm too tired to fight it directly.

OCTOBER 13, 2010

I went to a new counselor on Monday. I don't really know what to think of her yet. She's okay I guess. We'll see.

Christian and I were talking about her and how she asked what he thought of my weight. I told her that he liked me at any weight. Surprisingly, that wasn't as true as I thought. When we were talking about it he said something about still thinking that I'm pretty at this weight, but not liking it as much because he worries about me. Hm. He says I'm noticeably thinner. I don't think I look any different.

It's weird, even though I know that when I was super underweight I couldn't see it, it still seems like this time I'd notice if I'd lost weight. I guess that once again that's not the case. I don't know what to think anymore. I hate how I can't trust my own mind.

October 17, 2010

Tomorrow is my birthday. That doesn't actually mean much. We're not really doing anything to celebrate. The family dinner and dessert used to be special, but obviously not anymore. I'm just trying to use my birthday as something to look forward to. Something to get to. I'm going to be 18. That should be significant, right? It doesn't really feel that way. I mostly just feel old. My childhood is pretty much over. That makes me sad.

I'm meeting with that new counselor again tomorrow. I've missed the last two weeks of EDA [Eating Disorders Anonymous] meetings. I don't like them. They're too stressful.

October 26, 2010

Becky got really upset at dinner the other day. It was just Mom, Dad, her, and I. When I decided I had finished eating even though I still had some food on my plate, Mom said something about needing to eat more and I said no. Then Becky got all huffy and got up from the table really fast to dump her plate in the sink and run up the stairs. I called her overdramatic. Mom called her back to the table and said that she needed to share what she was feeling instead of bottling it in.

She was very reluctant, which is what first made me think that maybe she wasn't trying to be dramatic but was actually upset. I think she really was. I wish I had written about it right away so I'd remember more clearly, but she said something about not liking that I didn't finish. When Mom asked why, her answer surprised me. She said she didn't like seeing me go through this. Mom asked what it was that she didn't like seeing me go through and for some reason she had a really hard time saying eating disorder. She whined and complained, and then sort of mumbled it under her breath.

She is genuinely concerned about me. This really does upset her. I had thought (and hoped) that as the youngest all this would sort of go right over her head, but it hasn't/doesn't. This is hurting her. I'm hurting her. That makes me feel so horrible. I need to get better.

*   *   *

Grace taught me some common sense about food a couple nights later. Dinner again. Dinner is always the hardest. Grace said something about my food looking like it was dissected. I snapped back at her something about cutting up food and how everyone does it and that was all I was doing. She responded with, "Yeah, you cut it up... and then you eat it." That made me laugh. There's my problem! I've been forgetting the second step!

*   *   *

I'm taking baby steps toward recovery. I've come a long way from where I was a year ago, the darkest place I've ever been, but not always by my own effort or motivation. Those were the times that Christ carried me. Out from the darkness he carried me, when I was too weak and blind from the lies to stand on my own.

He has set me down in a better place. I'm stronger now, both physically and mentally. I see past the lies and often recognize the voice of the eating disorder. It is time I walk on my own. When I say on my own I of course don't really mean without Christ's help. I just mean that I am no longer being carried. I am taking tentative steps with Christ alongside me holding my hand. Jesus, thank you for being patient with me. I love you.

A Father's Perspective

The next two years consisted of various eating disorder clinics and treatments, some more effective than others. For Michelle and I, the experiences at each clinic that did not magically heal our daughter resulted in a strengthened resolve to do whatever was necessary to keep her alive. This resolve consumed us, taking over nearly every waking minute with research and monitoring of Justine's physical, emotional, and nutritional well-being. Michelle poured all her energy into learning about eating disorders. This constant attention to Justine and the eating disorder that gripped her so tightly took a toll on her three younger sisters, who were ages 8, 11, and 13 when she first became sick.

Michelle and I kept Justine's illness very private and only discussed it with a few people. We felt we were largely alone on this difficult journey. As a result, there were many moments of despair, of not knowing where to seek help. Despite these moments and the overall stress and anxiety that shrouded our family, Michelle and I remained closely united in the fight to save Justine. In fact, I would say we grew closer to each other and our marriage became stronger as a result of this journey. Fortunately, through what must have been divine intervention, we found a private counselor named Dana, with whom Justine really clicked.

This became the turning point in Justine's recovery, and we will be forever grateful to Dana for the impact she had on Justine.

October 28, 2010

It's Thursday today. On Monday while I was making my sandwich, I suddenly felt that I should purposely not make it in the usual order (mayo, cheese on that, chicken, and then cut with a new/clean knife). At first it just seemed silly, but then I realized that the fact that I had trouble doing it meant that it wasn't silly. The food ritual was important to me. Important to the eating disorder. It was safe.

So I did something unsafe. I put on the mayo first, then the chicken, then cheese, then cut it with the same knife I had used for the mayo. When I ate it, instead of ritualistically peeling off the crust, then the cheese, then eating the bread and chicken, I picked it up and ate it the normal way. It probably would seem strange to others that this is significant, but it was. It is. I've eaten my sandwich without ritual for the last four days.

When I saw Dana [the counselor I referred to] on Monday I told her about the sandwich thing and she said it was really good. She said it's important to break the rituals. I've been trying to do it some more this week. I usually eat my lunch in a certain order, but now I've been mixing it up. Instead of grapes, bar, sandwich at school and sandwich, grapes, bar at home, the last few days I've tried to make it more random. I even ate half my bar, then my sandwich, then the other half of my bar on Tuesday. I did the same thing with my banana and eggs Tuesday morning. Some banana, then some eggs, then some banana, then eggs. That tasted a little strange. I had the banana taste in my mouth while I was eating the eggs. I for sure think that the ritualistic preparation of the food needs to stop, but I don't know if the eating each food separate thing needs to stop. I've been doing that forever. That's not ED related except for at dinner when I eat all the good foods first so that if I leave food it will be the bad kind. Darn. I guess I'm not sure what to do with that piece of it.

On Monday Dana also said that a big part of recovery was being able to eat a variety of foods. Sometimes eating the same thing every day works out fine. Right now my school schedule and the fact that I live at home with my parents allows me to do that, but it won't always be that way. What about when I move out? Am I going to have access to the exact same foods as I did at home? Truthfully, the lack of variety has already kept me from doing things that I'd maybe like to do. I don't see my friends much anymore. They often get together around mealtimes, and I just don't feel comfortable eating what they're eating even if it's healthy food (then I'd be worried about portions). Sleepovers cause me a lot of anxiety even when I decide to have what they're having. They sleep in so darn late that it's time for lunch when they get up. If I wait until they wake up to eat breakfast with them, I end up having to cram all three meals into the afternoon. Gross. Sometimes I just leave early while they're still sleeping.

My eating disorder likes to tell me that the lack of variety is not a problem. Yeah, it's inconvenient, but it's just something that I have to deal with. No big deal. But really, it is a big deal. It's a huge deal. It handicaps me. I can't do anything with my friends if it's near any of my three meals (which is basically the whole day). When we travel or go on vacation my parents have to pack food for me. We can't go out to dinner as a family anymore. I can't do retreats or mission trips at church because I don't know what they'll serve. I feel awkward at family gatherings. They all know, but they don't say anything. I can't eat over at Christian's house when I'm invited. And what am I supposed to do when I'm off at college? Even if I'm living at home, I still won't be able to have the same foods if I want to be out doing stuff.

Living basically. Lack of variety is fine as long as I live at home my whole life and make sure that I'm there for every meal. As long as I stay inside my little bubble of safety and never experience God's real and beautiful plan for my life.

I had an egg sandwich (with meat) and an apple yesterday instead of the regular eggs, toast, and banana. It's not much, but it's a start. Dana wants me to try having at least one bite of dessert on my own (without someone telling me to). I've thought about it and planned it out mentally during the last few days, but haven't had the guts to follow through yet.

October 29, 2010

I had a peanut butter and jelly sandwich for lunch today. I decided on my own that I would have one. I haven't had peanut butter in a long time. It's on my bad list (was on my bad list?).

NOVEMBER 6, 2010

For a while I was seriously considering suicide. I had a plan and everything, but I knew I'd never really do it. I couldn't do that to my family. It was more of a fantasy than anything. I wanted so badly to end my pain, but I knew that it wasn't right. Sure my pain would end, but what about those who loved me? And yet the eating disorder. Isn't self-starvation just a slow form of suicide?

NOVEMBER 7, 2010

I know where Christ set me down. It was at the altar that day, months ago, when my eyes were really opened for the first time. When I truly let go of the eating disorder and placed it in God's hands. When I asked for his help. When I made the commitment, with his help, to get better.

NOVEMBER 8, 2010

The agreement we (Mom and I) made with Dana last Monday was that we'd only weigh once a week but I can see what's on the scale. Mom weighed me last Monday and I was ███ lb. It's been a really stressful week with not knowing.

I was supposed to take note of how I felt when we weighed again this morning. I was ███ lb. I feel a little relieved, happy even.

I can't help it. I was worried that I was gaining, so it's nice to know I wasn't. At the same time, I feel ugh when I think about it more. I do want to be healthy. A lower number just means that now I'll have to eat and gain even more. There. That's how I feel about it.

November 10, 2010

Tuesday and today I had two percent milk with lunch, and I've been trying to eat all of my food instead of leaving some (I haven't been doing well with that). I'm getting weighed tomorrow and I'm a little nervous.

November 14, 2010

My weight on Thursday (we decided to weigh halfway through the week so that we could catch it if it started to drop any more) was ▮lb. I don't know if I really gained a pound or if it was just a fluctuation, but at least it didn't go down.

Ahhhh, I'm so hungry, but no one is up. Someday I'll be able to go downstairs and get my own breakfast when I want it, but not yet.

November 16, 2010

Last Monday I asked Dana where the line was with weight in regards to okay versus hospitalization. She said that she had to think about/look into it before she got back to me. She told me yesterday ▮lb is when she'd be strongly suggesting inpatient. I thought it would be lower than that. I'm only 3lb away.

We did this weird perception test with an unmarked rope. I'm too tired to write anymore. I'll continue later.

November 18, 2010

When I was with Dana on Monday she had me take a rope and form a loop that I guessed was the same size as my stomach without measuring. I made one that I thought looked about right, and then made it even a little bit smaller because I figured that what I saw my waist as was probably a little bigger than what it really was.

It was bigger, but not a little. A lot. When she twisted the rope around my stomach there was a good six or seven inches extra. I was off by that much. Then she put her fingers on the place where the rope ends met and held them there when she pulled it off so that I could see how big the loop really was.

It was like a magic trick. When she first took out the rope she'd pulled it and asked if I wanted to feel it. She swore it wasn't a trick rope. I thought that was a little strange. Duh, it's not a trick rope. What are you talking about? But when she showed me the loop that was the size of my waist I understood. I couldn't help but wonder if it was a trick. My immediate reaction was disbelief. The thought "no one's stomach is that small" popped into my head. I couldn't, and still can't, wrap my head around it. It is so messed up.

Dana said that if I did the same rope test with a tissue box, I could probably get the rope pretty close to the actual size. She said that's because there's no emotion attached to the box. But when I look at myself, particularly the parts of my body that I don't like, I experience a lot of emotion that distorts the way I see it.

November 26, 2010

I don't remember exactly what it was that Mom said at dinner tonight. We were fighting about how much chili I had to eat. She said something about not wanting to talk to Ed and then something about my choosing... to get better maybe? To fight? I don't remember, but I replied with "since when have I ever had a choice?" and then promptly broke into tears. My own words hit hard. I think it was the first time I've ever cried about the eating disorder. The reality was/is too much. I am enslaved. It's supposedly all about control, but whose control? Not mine, that's for sure. I hate being a puppet. I want to be free.

November 28, 2010

After my breakdown at dinner the other night, Mom told me that she and Becky were talking about me. Becky said that she felt like she was watching her sister dying.

December 19, 2010

We added a denser type of bread [higher calorie content] to my meal plan. I had an extra granola bar as a snack for two weeks, but that didn't do anything so now we're trying something else. Well actually the bar did do something. I lost weight. Dana thinks it's because my metabolism kicked in. I think she's right. On the days that I had the bar I was actually hungrier than the days that I didn't. Now that we're adding, it seems like (can't say for sure) I'm hungry almost all the time. It's weird and I don't like it.

December 23, 2010

My weight is ▇▇lb—one pound away from the hospital. Merry Christmas. I don't get it. I've been pretty much following the plan. I have my denser bread with breakfast and lunch and a granola bar for snack. I'm not putting that much butter or mayo on my breads but I never have. I think I'll have to have a piece of peanut butter toast today instead of the usual granola bar. Mom says I have to change something. Ugh.

*   *   *

Mom and I went shopping yesterday before I went over to Christian's. We just went to pick out pajama pants, but we ended up looking at some other stuff too. It was really hard. Mom almost cried and I felt like crying. I really want new clothes, but I'm not supposed to get any when I'm at a bad weight. We got two shirts. Those should be okay if I gain. They're really cute. I'd like some new jeans though.

December 29, 2010

We added another snack to my meal plan on Monday. Now I'm having peanut butter toast in between breakfast and lunch and a granola bar between lunch and dinner.

Last night just as I was about to ask Christian if he thought that I would still look good if I gained weight, he wrapped his hand around one of my arms. Then he sighed disapprovingly and said that it was so thin. He says that I could gain a bunch of weight and still look good. Okay. Now I just have to keep reminding myself of that.

January 2, 2011

None of my clothes are fitting me right and it's driving me crazy. I'm so frustrated! I wanted to wear my silver shirt today, but I put on my black dress pants and they looked stupid. They're all baggy. I can't wear them with a tight shirt. So then, even though I don't like wearing jeans to church, I tried on my black jeans. They looked even worse. As Christian says, I'm too skinny for my skinny jeans. Ugh.

For a while after I had been at the day program, I had to deal with having a recovered body but not mind. Now I'm trying to work with the opposite. My mind is recovering but my body seems to be lagging behind. Sometimes I can even see what I look like. I'm too thin, I know that, and I'm trying to change it but it's so hard. I am so sick of these sunken cheeks! I want my round, pink cheeks back! (And I'm talking about the ones on my face of course. My butt still looks too big to me even though none of my pants are fitting.)

January 8, 2011

It's times like these that I feel I understand Christian the least. I just don't understand how anyone could love me or see me as beautiful. But he knows my flaws. He knows I have an eating disorder, depression, anxiety, and a horrible temper (though he hasn't seen that last in action yet). He knows that I cut, starve, make myself throw up. Still he loves me. I mean, I don't understand how God loves me either, but that's different. He's God. Christian is human and he loves me.

God, that is one amazing young man you have created. I don't know your plans for the future, or if our futures are intertwined, but either way thank you. Thank you for our friendship and the relationship we have right now. Thank you for bringing him into my life just when I needed a friend the most. Thank you for teaching him to love. Please teach that love to me as well. Help me to love you first so that I can know perfect love and then love others. Your will, always, be done. My life is yours. All that I am, I am not without you. I love you.

January 9, 2011

Either I'm losing weight or my eyes are starting to work for the first time in a while. It's still not all the time, but often I see myself as thin. Too thin. I don't look at myself naked before I get into the shower like some people do. I'm still way too vulnerable to the eating disorder's lies to do that. I'm afraid of what I'd see. But sometimes if I'm in the bathroom changing or just wearing a tank top I look. Sometimes I can see.

I see my ribs and, more recently, the bones at my chest. I wonder if my cheekbones and jaw are supposed to be that sharp and defined. I don't think they are in my old pictures. I can stick my fingers in under my chin and feel the inside of my jaw bone. It that normal? If I turn my back to the mirror and hunch my shoulders a little bit I can clearly see my entire rib cage. My arms look abnormally thin when I do that too.

I try not to do that too much though because the eating disorder gets a grotesque sort of pleasure from it. I don't understand what that pleasure and fascination from seeing human bones is all about. It's a dark pleasure though. I know that.

It's the same sort of pleasure I feel when I think about bodily injuries and blood. I've seen pictures of really emaciated people before. Just recently in a book I was reading and an especially shocking picture in my history class. It was really hard to believe that the people in the pictures were alive. How could they be? I've seen pictures of really sick anorexics before too, and they were nothing like this. These people looked like skeletons that someone had crudely pasted skin onto. It was horrible, and yet I was fascinated. I wanted to touch them. To trace each individual bone with my fingers and stick my hand into each unnatural crevice to feel the bone's underside as well. Even more strongly, I wanted to be them. To be in their body. To have it be mine. To feel myself like that. To have each bone I trace be mine. I was jealous. How sick is that?

There's something seductive about the idea of touching death. Of walking a line between the living and the dead. It's a part of the eating disorder. One of its pulls and maybe, in the end, it's only pull. When I came out of the bathroom once after dance practice with just spandex and a sports bra on, Dad told me that I looked like someone from a concentration camp. "Emaciated," he said. Mom and Whitney cried. I find it hard to believe that I could have looked anything like those pictures, the really bad ones at least, but really we were in a similar place. Not living but not dead either. A sort of middle world. Maybe the differences balance each other out. Their bodies were in worse condition, but their minds were focused on living. They fought death while I embraced it. I really can't say which is more dangerous.

I remember that place though. The middle world. The darkest place I have ever been. I remember being so underweight that each step was an effort. The hallways at school seemed to stretch on forever. I couldn't look up or I'd get discouraged. I could only stare at my feet, smiling and nodding to what everyone else was saying and trying to appear normal as I struggled with each step. Dance practice was torture. I had no energy. Every time I stretched, spun, or jumped (anything that required a little extra push of effort) my vision darkened, the blood rushed to my head, and I saw stars. I still frequently have nightmares about being too thin for my legs to support me. In my dreams I struggle to walk, and eventually my twig-like legs buckle and collapse underneath me.

My mind was not among the living. It floated instead in that middle world. Lost in the darkness. Eventually everything, even the pain of depression, vanished. I felt nothing. I was nothing. Nothing but an empty shell where my spirit had once been. Thoughts of death were my only comfort, and I'm not over exaggerating when I say that it was almost all I thought about. Death and pain. I fantasized about them both constantly. I thought about all the different types of ways to cause pain (guns, knives, matches, etc.) and then imagined what that pain would feel like. I thought about dying and the different ways to die. I thought about suicide. I plotted my own multiple times. The ideal method, in my mind, was to die in a way that would not cause my family to suspect that I'd been trying to die. I didn't want them to have to deal with all the what-ifs and self-blame that usually follows a suicide.

Though I thought about it a lot and actually did come up with a sort of final plan, I always knew that I'd never really kill myself. Now with a clearer head, I can say that I'd rather go through the most painful life possible than cause my loved ones to suffer. With my mind in such darkness though, I wasn't thinking that way at all. All I wanted was the pain to end. My friends would get over it, I decided. My family was strong enough to deal with it and, if my plans worked out, wouldn't even know it was a suicide. Even God I was willing to face. I knew he'd be disappointed in me, but I also felt strongly that he would understand my pain and be merciful.

Christian, on the other hand, I could not face. I felt very strongly that I could not put him through that. I can't say why exactly. Because he loved me was the biggest reason, but my family loved me too and I wasn't going to let that stop me. It was different with him for some reason. I don't even know if we were going out yet, but I knew how he felt about me. I guess I felt that if I died I would take a part of him with me. I didn't want that. Sometimes I wanted to hate him for being what I believed was the one thing that kept me alive. But of course I couldn't really ever hate him. God knew what he was doing when he gave me

Christian as a lifeline. I can't imagine that anything else would have had as much influence.

[To those who have lost a loved one to suicide: Please know that I do not want to imply in any way that if your family member, friend, or significant other had loved you they would not have ended their life. As a teenager I wrote some pretty bold statements about not committing suicide because of my family and Christian. But these journal entries were *not* written when I was feeling my worst. They were written later when I actually felt good enough to journal. In hindsight, of course I felt that way. I believed suicide was wrong, but I also believed that self-harm was wrong and I still resorted to that. When I was hurting, the pain was the only thing I could think about. If it had been any more intense or lasted any longer, my story might have ended differently.]

January 11, 2011

We did a weigh-in yesterday and I was ▇lb. That's the highest it's been in a while, so I guess the new meal plan is working. We did a blind weigh-in on Thursday and I'm really glad because Mom said it was ▇lb then too and that probably would have freaked me out. Since it was still ▇lb four days later, I'm okay with it. I know I'm not gaining 2lb every few days. I am heading in the right direction though.

January 16, 2011

I feel so incredible. Better than I've felt in a long long time. The last two days have been so great. Nothing in particular has happened. I've mostly just been doing homework and hanging out at home. Whitney had a cheer competition yesterday that I went to (they won third place) and then she and I went to mass. But I've just felt so so good. I feel happy. Happy! I'm happy! I almost want to cry with relief. Sometimes I wondered if I'd ever feel happy again. Thank you God. Thank you, thank you! I know it won't be like this forever, but I also know that when I'm depressed I won't be like that forever either. Thank you God for this precious moment and the joy that is bubbling up inside of me.

Note to future self: No matter how dark it may seem at times, don't forget that it will not last forever. Just keep pushing until you've gone as far as you can go, and then push some more. Don't ever stop praising and thanking God.

I feel hope. Tons of it. When I look toward the future I don't see emptiness. I see endless possibilities. I've always known that God has a plan for me, but I never really *knew* it until now. He has a plan for me! Thank you God. I am ready to follow wherever you lead.

* * *

I went to a healing mass on Wednesday (the 12th). Christian and my parents were asked to play music and they both said I should go. It was pretty nice. Fr. James talks a lot (not that that's a bad thing). The line to get prayed over after mass was huge. I waited because I didn't want to go before anyone else. That would've felt wrong. We are all already, as humans, unworthy of God's love and healing. I felt that if I was to get healed at all it should be after everyone else. Mom and I were there until eleven. Fr. James prayed over each of us.

I can't say if I was healed the moment he prayed over me. But I do know that I will be healed. That God will heal me. I believe it now more strongly than I ever have before. Someday I will be free.

* * *

I had some brownie this afternoon. This morning before church Becky claimed the extra brownie and I finally told them how that makes me feel—like they think I'll never get better. Then I had it for snack. (They promised not to do that anymore.)

January 22, 2011

I went to Feed My Starving Children [a nonprofit that prepares and ships dehydrated meals to children in third world countries] with Becky. While I was there I had some really disturbing eating disorder thoughts. Its voice is definitely still there (or maybe it has trained me so well that I've subconsciously taken over for it. I don't know). I started comparing myself to the pictures of the malnourished children. It still hurts to look. I feel compassion for them, but at the same time there's this little voice inside me that ignores the misery in their eyes and says "Ha! I can see my ribs too!" I still feel the familiar yet disturbing pang of jealousy. The before and after pictures were amazing. I immediately thanked God for restoring that sickly little baby to health, but at the same time I was terrified. The voice says, "Oh shit. You can gain that much weight in 16 days?" (or however long it was).

I hate that voice. It has no regard for human health or happiness. It places no value on human life. It's evil. It's the opposite of everything I am called to be, but I've been with it for too long and it's become a part of me. I am ready to fight it though. To get rid of it. I can't do it alone.

"For although we are in the flesh, we do not battle according to the flesh." - 2 Corinthians 10:3 [New American Bible]

This battle is a spiritual one. I am not alone because Christ and all he commands is on my side. Lord, I am ready for battle. I am ready to reclaim my soul and all that rightly belongs to you. I am not a warrior yet, but trust that you can teach me and will lead me.

January 27, 2011

I am so hungry. I hate being hungry. I can't focus. Its six o'clock now and I don't know what time dinner will get done, but I probably won't get any schoolwork finished until it is. Ugh. I hate hate hate this feeling. It brings back bad memories. At least now I'll (eventually, when dinner is done) be able to eat. Before I could only pick at my food even while starving.

January 30, 2011

Mom was telling me about this woman from church the other day that sent her a card. She told Mom that she was praying for different people and Mom kept coming to mind. Then she woke up in the middle of the night and thought of Mom and then the words "past," "gone," and "healing".

February 12, 2011

I think the eating disorder is gone. That doesn't mean I'm back to the way I was before. It took two years to teach me, so my mind often fills in with what it would have said, but I don't think its presence is here anymore. It can't be because God has opened my eyes and I see it for what it really is. It has no hold over me anymore. Sometimes I feel it trying to sneak back in, but so far it hasn't worked. God's light reveals truth, and with his help I am able to drive the eating disorder away or at least keep it from getting back in. Thank you God for freeing me. Now all that's left is to work on the thoughts that it has conditioned to appear in certain circumstances and recognize that my human eyes don't always see truth when I look into the mirror. Lord, through you I can do all things. Help me to know truth. Mold my thoughts and keep my heart fixed on you. Help me to recognize and fight the eating disorder when it tries to push its way back into my life.

FEBRUARY 14, 2011

I had a sort of epiphany the other day. I guess it makes sense and I kind of knew it all along, but I didn't really realize until now. When I'm not hungry I don't think about food as much. It's not the actual feeling of hunger it's the definition of it—a need or desire for food. So I guess a person can be hungry without feeling it. When I was extremely underweight I stopped feeling hunger, but my body was still hungry and I constantly thought about food. I smelled it, touched it, stared at it in magazine ads, cooked it, fantasized about it, and dreamt about it at night. I did pretty much everything possible with it except what my body really wanted me to do: eat it.

Looking back on it now I want to laugh, or cry, or both maybe. How could I not have realized what my body was trying to tell me the entire time? I needed food, and that's why all of my thoughts and actions revolved around it.

MARCH 15, 2011

I am so ready to be done with the eating disorder. It keeps me from God, so I want it gone. All of it. Every single little piece of it left in my life. Here are my goals (I met some of them this week):

- Eat something (probably a dessert) voluntarily (At my cousin's birthday party last Sunday I had a bowl of ice cream. Then for Whitney's birthday I had some of her pie even though it was disgusting.)
- Eat dinner with Christian's family (Did it yesterday. Wasn't weird at all. Enchiladas. Yum.)
- Go to Chipotle with Christian
- Go out to eat with my family
- Have a slice of restaurant pizza
- Eat something my girlfriends are snacking on voluntarily
- Eat one McDonalds French fry (got to start small)
- Have a hot dog
- Have a serving of homemade French fries

- Have a spoonful of cookie dough or other batter (to show myself I won't go crazy and eat the whole bowl)
- Have a glass of pop (non-diet)

MARCH 19, 2011

Whitney, Grace, Becky, Mom, and I went to the Mall of America yesterday. It was actually tons of fun even though we only shopped the entire time (I hate shopping). Everyone was in a really good mood. We went to Bubba Gump's for lunch so I met one of my goals (eating out). Choosing what to order was the hard part. It wasn't too bad after that.

* * *

Today my doubts about our [Christian and my] relationship popped up again. I was already a little bit distressed (we had just watched *The Green Mile*) and then suddenly I started thinking about our relationship and my anxiety level hit the ceiling. It was so random. I'd had such a great, depression-free week, and then all of a sudden I was all shaky and nervous and then burst into tears. Christian just held me while I cried. When I asked him if he was prepared to deal with random outbursts like that for the rest of his life his yes was immediate.

March 21, 2011

I was amazed that when we were at the mall on Saturday I could see people and not just bodies. It was so nice. Thank you God.

March 23, 2011

Christian and I went to Chipotle yesterday! Another goal crossed off the list. It was really great. That's the first dinner date we've ever had. It was super fun, and the burrito even tasted pretty good too. The look on Becky's face when I told her Christian and I were going out to eat was priceless (though it makes my heart ache to think about it now). I think she was trying to act normal, but her grin gave her away. If someone who didn't know us walked into Mom and Dad's room at the moment I came in to tell them, if they heard me say "Christian and I are going out to eat" casually and then witnessed our smiles, they would have thought they'd missed some sort of inside joke. It was great. A year ago I doubted that recovery was even possible (for me at least). Just look at what God has done and is continuing to do to me now!

For a while I was gaining. Slowly, but still gaining. These last two weeks I've stayed pretty much stable even though I've been working really hard with my meal plan. Today was the first time I've ever lost weight and felt only frustration (without any hint of delight). I groaned when I saw the number.

* * *

So much has been going on lately. I just can't keep up with it all (with journaling I mean). The days are so long, but not in a bad way. They're just so eventful that sometimes when I look back on the morning it's hard to believe that it's the same day. I see and learn new things every day now. It's wonderful. I suppose that's what happens when you're blind and then can see.

I'm remembering things too, and really seeing them for the first time. Driving by Subway today brought back memories of a dream I had. I told Mom about it while sitting in the car in front of that very restaurant. In the dream, I was standing in front of Jesus holding an apple from the tree of life (that had been bitten from) and I was wrapped in something. I believe it was a snake. Bound is probably a better word, not wrapped. I was blind and I didn't even acknowledge Jesus standing in front of me. He gently took the apple from my hand and then held up the Eucharist.

The peculiar thing about this vision is that it happened before the eating disorder had gotten bad. Really, it was just beginning. I saw truth. I knew it for a second, but I still fell. Inside the restaurant I asked something of Mom that she would never let me forget. As the last pieces of myself fought against the darkness that was trying to drag me under, I begged her not to give up on me. To keep fighting when I no longer could and even when I turned against her. She promised she would, and she did.

May 19, 2011

I see it now. I was making everything so complex in my head, but it is actually very simple. Incredibly simple. The meaning of life, of existence. There's probably millions of books written on it. People look at it as if it is some sort of huge, complex puzzle that only the smartest can figure out. Yet toddlers act in a way that suggests that they are aware of it. It's the simple who really know it best. It can be summed up in one word: him.

Complex can't even begin to describe God. Incomprehensible is better. He himself we are not capable of understanding, but our hearts know him and our job, our meaning, is simple: living for him.

For a moment my eyes are open and I see truth. The truth. Jesus. My lack of understanding about the spiritual realm is irrelevant. He is all that matters. All that I have to do is abandon myself to his will. Then I don't have to worry about anything ever. He will guide me. He will take care of me. If there's some knowledge that I need in order to fulfill his will then he will make it known to me and I don't have to fry my brain trying to understand it on my own because I never could anyway. Simple but beautiful. Jesus, I love you.

June 2, 2011

Every day is a battle. Life is so much easier and harder than it ever has been before (yep it's possible). It's amazing how many ups and downs I experience in a single day. Exhausting but worth it. Sometimes I can't help but wonder if anyone else lives like this. The days seem so easy for other people, so why is it that if mine were a minute longer I might not make it through? I suppose it doesn't really matter anyway. It is how it is.

June 18, 2011

On Thursday for the church's 30th anniversary Fr. Thomas gave a talk. He gave us a scripture passage to read through and told us to stop at whatever struck us and meditate on it. It was Luke 19, the story of Zacchaeus. I started to think that nothing would strike me. Then I hit the very last verse: "For the Son of Man has come to seek and to save what was lost" [Luke 19:10, New American Bible]. My heart melted. To seek and to save what was lost. I was lost, and he didn't just sit around waiting for me to return to him. He sought me. Found me. Saved me. He rescued me because he loves me (Psalm 18).

The following image came to mind: I was walking across the sea towards the kingdom on the other side. Jesus was walking alongside me holding my hand. I'm not sure if I saw the waves first or let go of his hand, but either way I started to sink and then, when I did not reach out to him as I should have, plunged into the water.

I couldn't swim. I'd thought I knew how, but I didn't. Even as I flailed about and took in mouthfuls of water, I kept telling myself that I could make it on my own. I didn't need him. That's what the water was whispering even as it slowly drew me under. The entire time Jesus crouched beside me with his arms outstretched, but I ignored him and wouldn't reach out to him. A few times I started to, but I got scared because to do so I had to stop paddling and give up the little bit of control that I thought I had.

Then, quite suddenly, I sunk. I'd thought that I was doing fine on my own but I was wrong. By the time I realized that I wasn't and never had been in control it was too late. I was already under and I was drowning. Did I actually cry out or did I just give one last longing glance at the surface? I don't remember. What I do remember is that Christ did not give up on me. He dove in and found me in the darkness. Snatched me from the grave (Psalm 107). Then he brought me back to life (what wondrous love). Now we walk upon the waves hand in hand again, and he will not let me fall (Psalm 37).

June 27, 2011

I'm ready to be done with any type of food routine (eating disorder related). It's going to be tough, but I believe that's what God's asking of me and I am trying to trust. He would never ask me to do something and then abandon me.

June 30, 2011

On Monday Dana gave me the okay to get rid of the meal plan (having the same things all the time). It's Thursday today and so far it's been going really well. I have so much extra time when I don't have to worry about food. I've been taking it one meal or snack at a time and trying to trust that my body will let me know what it needs.

August 20, 2011

My anxiety level concerning food and weight keeps going up and up this week. I've been doing really well. I've been barely thinking about food or weight lately, and at my last meeting with Dana we decided to stop doing blind, mid-week weigh-ins and meet only once every three weeks. Since Thursday though, I've been having a really hard time. I hung out with my friends Thursday night and had three little brownie muffins, two cheetos, and five pizza rolls. Obviously not much of a big deal for anyone else (Christian chuckled when I told him I had five whole pizza rolls!), but it was a push for me.

It wasn't much of a problem Thursday, but on Friday I had a bit of trouble keeping up with regular meals because I was tempted to eat less to make up for the night before. Dana had encouraged me to do some challenges too (she suggested something like having pizza twice in one day), so that evening for my night snack instead of the usual I had banana bread. My thought was that I would take on one of the things I find the most difficult: eating challenging foods multiple days in a row. Today (Saturday) I had a big burger for dinner and a piece of chocolate cake. Now my anxiety is going crazy. It's really really bad. I still have three more days before another weigh-in and I am extremely nervous. I'm going to have a lot of trouble with the anxiety for the next two days.

We're in the car now on the way home from my cousins' house. I was just praying about it. I asked that the Lord take this anxiety from me. The problem is that I keep grabbing onto it. I know that he wants me to turn the anxieties over to him the moment they pop up, and I want to, but I have a lot of trouble actually doing it. I think part of it is that I've entertained the anxieties for so long that often I let them in automatically without thinking about it. I have to learn to catch them at the beginning right when they first come up.

September 4, 2011

I've been finding out recently that Whitney was more strongly affected by the eating disorder than I had imagined. She is so good at hiding her feelings. This hurts me so much. Lord I am so so sorry! I never meant to hurt anyone, but I hurt all the people that love me the most. Lord, only you can right these wrongs and fix the effects of the mistakes I have made. Please do so. I am so sorry. It kills me to think about how much I have hurt the very people I love the most. Sometimes I think that it would have been better if I had died some other way before this whole thing started. But Lord only you can see the full picture. If it weren't for your goodness and mercy I would have never been healed or, even if I had, been able to live with the guilt of what I'd done. But you, my God, have cast my sins from me as far as the East is from the West (Psalm 103). If I have all eternity to sing your praises it will still be nothing compared to what you have done for me. You have given me everything. You have given me life.

September 11, 2011

Today's readings during mass were really great. They were about forgiveness and how God has forgiven us so we must in turn forgive others. This brought up some past hurts for me. I realized that even though I had told God that I had forgiven those who hurt me (the people who saw what the eating disorder was doing to me and never said anything), whenever I thought or talked about them it was bitterly, so once again I came before God, lifted them up to him, and forgave them.

During the homily, Fr. Thomas brought up something that really surprised me. He said that when the Bible talks about forgiveness it's not just talking about us forgiving others. It's also talking about us forgiving ourselves. God has forgiven us. If we still hold a grudge against ourselves then, it's like we're doubting the power of his mercy.

September 30, 2011

Tuesday was my last meeting with Dana. She doesn't think I need her anymore. I've graduated (as Dad says) from eating disorder therapy. I can check off all the boxes on the "what does recovery look like" paper that she gave me. It looks like this.

October 19, 2011

I think I might have overeaten a little tonight. Dad made coffee ice cream cake and it was really good, but (as much as the eating disorder is trying to sneak in and convince me otherwise) I did not go out of control. Dad cut me a really big piece. I ate some of it and felt a little full, and then I made the conscious decision to eat a little more because it was really good. I know that people don't gain weight by overeating once. It has to happen repetitively and over a period of time. I think this is a pretty big accomplishment for me. I've thought about it a couple of times tonight, but I haven't been overly anxious.

December 19, 2011

I was cleaning out my room today and I found an old razor blade stashed inside a little ceramic baby shoe that my parents gave me when I was an infant. It's amazing how much things have changed. I used to hide blades all over my room in case my parents found one of them and took it away. I was terrified of the possibility of being left with nothing to cut with. I didn't know how else to cope. That feels like a dream now. A lifetime away.

JANUARY 28, 2012

Change can be scary. It involves letting go of something.

1 YEAR LATER

December 23, 2012

I went shopping with Whitney today after church. She was going to a crafty store and a bookstore so I figured it wouldn't be that bad even though I don't usually like to shop. We got to talk quite a bit in the car, which was part of the reason I went actually. I haven't talked to her in a while. I don't even see her that much. It was really nice. I'm going to miss her so much when she moves out.

Our talking eventually landed on the topic of healthy eating and exercise. Whitney said that she hates that I'm working out again. Every time I go down to the basement to work out it brings back bad memories and she said she wants to run down there, rip off my tennis shoes, and march me back up the stairs. She'd prefer that I never exercise again. I explained that it helps with the depression and that I'm being careful. She said she knows (of course) that it's good for you, but it still makes her uncomfortable. "I'm not going to let you die," she said. I smiled, but she was serious. She made me promise that I would ask for help if I ever started slipping. I promised, and then she made me pinky swear.

Certain, powerful moments with her are frozen in my memory. That moment, sitting in the front of her car with our pinkies and eyes locked, will be one of them. My heart aches with love and remorse for the pain I know that I have caused her. If I could take it back I would. It's the only thing in my life that I would redo if I had the choice.

December 30, 2012

For a while when I looked toward the future I saw nothing. Blank. And then I felt depressed. Despair. Things must have changed slowly because I didn't notice them changing. It suddenly hit me today how different my view of the future is. When I look toward the future now I see endless possibilities. I'm excited! I know that God has some amazing things in store for me and that excites me. He has been moving in incredible ways and I'm excited to see him do so even more in the future. My hope. My joy. Thank you. For everything.

January 28, 2013

God is so amazing. You'd think I'd eventually stop being surprised when crazy things happen and prayers (even those unspoken) are answered in unexpected but wonderful ways.

I had planned on confronting Christian yesterday (we're not good for each other, what do you see in me, etc., etc.; the usual), but after praying about it I decided not to. I felt that it would demonstrate a lack of faith in the fact that God knows what he's doing.

When I got home later that night there was a letter waiting for me on the counter. A letter that I had written to myself while I was in Guatemala [I had done a study abroad program through the university I attended] that the program coordinator had promised to send us six months after we got back. I got goose bumps reading it. It was exactly what I needed to hear. I wrote about how, at the time of the letter, I knew nothing about the future but it was okay. And if six months later when I read the letter I still didn't know, it would still be okay. "Every day," I wrote, "God is teaching me a little more about trust," and he taught me there that "he is the only one I need.... I had my own plans for the future when I came here, but God totally destroyed them (thank you God). Now the only thing I am sure of is him. It's okay though. I am at peace." And the peace that found me there has found me here. At the end of the note I wrote "I have loved life here without the eating disorder and anxiety, and I don't want them when I go back. I'm done." I needed that. I had forgotten.

February 12, 2013

I had a really bad episode on Friday. [In mental health, the term "episode" is often used to describe a flare-up of symptoms. It can be over a short or a long period of time. When I use the term here I am referring to a very short time period (minutes or hours rather than days) in which my depression symptoms got so bad that I could no longer function.] I was the closest I've come to hurting myself in a long time. I really thought I was going to do it. I didn't feel like I had any other option. I was crying hysterically and couldn't get my breathing under control. I was on my way to school and my class was starting in fifteen minutes. I thought "If I get there, still can't stop, and class is going to start I'll need to do it." The cigarette lighter was in my car. I knew that one really good burn (not from the side but straight on, full circle, and pressed in) would stop the inner turmoil. I also knew that God wouldn't be thrilled, but I assumed that he would understand. I honestly didn't see any other option.

But then I thought about the guilt I would feel afterwards and how hard it would be to start over again from square one. There is no such thing as "just this once" with addictions. As my car passed by the woods I opened the window and threw the lighter as hard as I could. I thought I would feel better then with the temptation gone but actually I felt much worse. I felt the same way when I threw out my razors. I kept thinking about getting them out of the trash. When I drove home on Friday I kept an eye out for the lighter, half hoping I wouldn't find it and half hoping I would. I didn't. I don't regret what I did.

I'm fine today. Good actually. The weirdest, and probably the most dangerous, part of depression is its ability to convince you that how you feel now is how you've always felt and how you will always feel. When I'm not in an episode I know this is a lie, but when I'm in one it gets me every time. Despair is a poison.

1 Year Later

March 23, 2014

I used to think that the darkness I sometimes experience was caused by sin. I don't worry about that much anymore though. And isn't it action that matters anyway? In the end, my emotions don't always mean much. They're just chemical reactions in my brain. It's what I do or don't do about the emotions now that will matter. My brain is broken.

As a result, I sometimes feel emotional pain when there is no reason for it, but I don't need to act on that pain or feed into the lies about its causes (e.g., you're worthless, your relationship with Christian will never work, etc.). There is obviously physical factors involved in this struggle, but I believe that there are spiritual factors also. The pain is real, but the reasons that I come up with (because my logic tells me that if there is pain then there must be a reason for it) are not. When the depression first started in seventh grade, I was convinced that the pain was from a broken heart. Maybe though (it was so long ago that I don't really remember), the pain actually came first and I attributed it to what was happening in my environment. Every teenage girl suffers rejection at some point, but they get over it. They don't spend every night crying in the bathroom. They don't have fits of anger that mask the pain. They don't develop eating disorders and self-harm. My thoughts of worthlessness fed on the pain, and the pain grew when I ruminated on thoughts about being too ugly, too fat, too shy, etc. It was a vicious cycle.

Oh my gosh! For the first time I can see. Thank you God! They are all lies! For all these years I have been believing lies. The pain is just pain. There is no reason for it. It is not my subconscious mind telling me that there is something wrong with me. I am not ugly or fat or stupid. I am not worthless. I am made in God's image and I am beautiful. I'm good. I am smart and funny. God thank you, thank you, thank you! Please don't let me forget this. Don't let me slip back to where I was before. I don't want to be blind anymore. I am done with the lies. I want to see. I want truth. God, I want you.

August 28, 2014

suffering = pain + nonacceptance

I work so hard to change my pain that I can't also accept it. Therefore I suffer. None of these things that I throw myself into to change the depression fix it. If they help at all it's only for a moment, and then I'm back to suffering because nothing has really changed. It's going to be very difficult, but what I really need to do is work on accepting the depression.

Yes, it sucks that I have it because it's painful, but there's most likely nothing that can be done to cure it so I'll just have to learn to live with it. The dark times come and go, but they never last forever. There are good times too, even though the depression tries to convince me otherwise. I can acknowledge the urges for self-harm (or other destructive behaviors), the low energy, and the lack of motivation when they come up. Acknowledge them, and then move on. Act skillfully anyway. Do what I don't feel like doing even though it's hard.

September 14, 2014

I often forget how close I came to dying. Then out of nowhere and for no apparent reason, the memories come flooding back. I sometimes think I feel bad now, I still struggle with the depression and anxiety occasionally, but it is nothing compared to where I've come from. A living hell. The walking dead. The memories almost make me sick. Throwing food in the trash cans at school. Trying to make it down the hallway on twig legs. Watching the cracks on the floor and making each new one my new goal because I couldn't possibly make it all the way to the end. Bringing a day's worth of homework downstairs to avoid having to go back up because that single flight of stairs was so difficult. My vision going black and seeing stars every time I tried to do the cartwheel that was a part of our routine in dance class. The shifting mirrors—one moment seeing nothing but fat and the next horrified by sunken cheeks and a skeletal frame. Writing "fuck you" on my stomach and a yelling match and physical struggle with my parents the day they dragged me to the treatment center. Sitting with the two of them at the dinner table long after my half-eaten food had grown cold because they wouldn't let me leave until I ate.

They never gave up on me, even long after I had given up on myself. They worked so hard to keep me alive. I can't let that be wasted. I need to fight this and to keep fighting this no matter what.

OCTOBER 15, 2014

There's a reason why I went through what I did. I don't think about it often, but lately my story has been bubbling to the surface of my consciousness. Not many people know about it yet, but I think that the time to share is coming.

A Father's Perspective

It has now been seven or eight years since Justine was at her lowest point. Some of the painful details have faded from my memory, although I doubt this is true for Justine. I am proud of Justine for fighting through this horrific illness and for trusting in her mom and me. I'm sure there were so many times that trust was the last thing Justine wanted to do, but she did. In the end, it was Justine who had to decide herself to take down Ed, the eating disorder. We could not make her fight. She had to make that decision on her own.

Justine is doing well now although, as much as I would like to, I can't say for sure that she will ever be 100% free of the eating disorder. I suspect that she is more aware of certain triggers and now knows how to respond to these. While I certainly wish the eating disorder had never happened to Justine, I do think it strengthened her and helped shape her into who she is today: a remarkably strong, resilient, and very talented young lady with a future of endless possibilities in front of her.

A Mother's Perspective

One day I heard a song on the radio that became my hope. The song is called, "If You Want Me To," by Ginny Owens.[5] Part of the song says, "I will go through the valley if you want me to." I had found myself walking through a dark valley as I walked with Justine in her illness. It gave me strength to know that the Lord was with me.

Justine and I have talked about that chapter of her life. Now that she is well on the road to recovery, we can look back at those times and talk about how they changed us. It has made our friendship as mother and daughter a unique bond. I wouldn't trade that aspect of the journey for anything. It has also brought me into a deeper relationship with my Lord. I could not have gone through that time in my life without him.

I want to offer hope to you as you read these words. There is pain and suffering with this dreadful illness, but there is also hope for recovery. Hold onto that. Keep working to fight for yourself or for your loved one. When you feel like you no longer have the energy to do that on your own, lean on the Lord and let him give you the strength you need.

A Future Full of Hope

"For I know well the plans I have in mind for you, says the Lord, plans for your welfare and not for woe, plans to give you a future full of hope" –Jeremiah 29:11 [New American Bible]

I've met a lot of people with eating disorders, both during my own treatment and in my work in the mental health field. One common thread I've noticed with every person I've talked to is that the disorder has very little to do with actual food. It also rarely exists as a single diagnosis. My symptoms of depression began in early adolescence, years before the eating disorder, and my anxiety had been around for as long as I can remember. Though these journal entries focused mainly on the eating disorder, I hope that the underlying problems were apparent as well since I believe they are at the core of what caused the eating disorder symptoms. I stopped seeing Dana in September of 2011, but I met with a different therapist to work on depression and anxiety for a full year afterward.

As far as where I am today, well I'm at a place that at one point I didn't think was possible. It's been years since I've had any eating disorder symptoms. I'm still cautious, because I know relapses happen, but right now I'm doing great. I try to eat healthy, but I don't stress too much about it. I still enjoy dark chocolate and turtle mochas from the coffee shop every so often. I started weight training a few years ago and found that I love it, but I limit myself to two or three one-hour sessions a week. For the first time in my life I actually like my body most days. On the days when I'm feeling bloated I accept it, knowing that body fluctuations are a normal thing and I still can't always trust my perception of myself when I'm in a bad mood.

I wish I could say that the depression and anxiety are a thing of the past as well, but that's not always the case. It is different though. The symptoms occur only every so often, more like getting the flu than something I'm constantly carrying around. When I am feeling depressed or anxious it's still miserable, and I still have to fight the lie that "this is how things have always been and always will be," but now during these episodes my own voice is stronger than it was. It's pushing back against that lie with the reminders of my good days and the promise that it won't always be this way.

And still, years down the road, I have my support system of family and friends. Christian and I were married in 2014. We live close to our families and see them often. I finished a master's degree in counseling in 2016. Although I am currently working outside the field, mental health issues are still something I am passionate about, and I strongly believe that both my educational background and personal experience will serve a future purpose.

Please know, dear reader, that the fight is so worth it. I know that sometimes it feels like there is no hope, no future, and that even if there were it wouldn't be possible to get there through the pain. I'm writing to tell you that it is possible. There is hope. And you can make it. You can't do this alone, but there are those waiting to help you. Please reach out for the help you need and continue to fight for the future you'll have.

Notes

Back Cover

1. Hudson, James I., et al. "The Prevalence and Correlates of Eating Disorders in the National Comorbidity Survey Replication." *Biological Psychiatry*, vol. 61, no. 3, 2007, pp. 348–358.

2. Grange, Daniel Le, et al. "Eating Disorder Not Otherwise Specified Presentation in the US Population." *International Journal of Eating Disorders*, vol. 45, no. 5, 2012, pp. 711–718.

3. Smink, Frédérique R. E., et al. "Epidemiology of Eating Disorders: Incidence, Prevalence and Mortality Rates." *Current Psychiatry Reports*, vol. 14, no. 4, 2012, pp. 406–414.

May 26, 2009 Entry

4. The Maudsley Approach is a family-based eating disorder treatment approach in which parents play an active role in first restoring the teen's weight to prevent the negative side effects associated with severe malnutrition and then help the teen gain healthy control over their own eating. For a more detailed description of this approach, see

Treatment Manual for Anorexia Nervosa: A Family-Based Approach by James Lock and Daniel Le Grange.

A Mother's Perspective

5. Owens, Ginny. "If You Want Me To." *Without Condition*, Rocketown Records, 2006.

In loving memory of Michelle Gelineau

April 2, 1966 – July 10, 2018

This book would never have been possible without you. You're the reason I'm alive to tell my story and the one who always encouraged me to share it. I only wish you were here to see it finished.

I love you Mom.

Made in the USA
Coppell, TX
18 March 2021